All about the Jack Russell Terrier

Vicar of Swymbridge 1832/1880

Rev: John Russell.

All about the Jack Russell Terrier

MONA HUXHAM

Drawings by Caroline Haffner

PELHAM BOOKS

Stephen Greene Press

To Decimal Point who showed me first,
in 1946, the delights and drawbacks of being
owned by one of these remarkable little terriers
and to her sons Toff and Chum who,
for fourteen and thirteen years respectively,
gave me and my husband's family a wonderful
companionship full of pleasure and interest.

"Ay see the Hounds with frantic zeal
    The roots and earth uptear
    But the earth is strong
    And the roots are long
    They cannot enter there:
    Outspeaks the Squire "Give room I pray
    And hie the terriers in;
    The warriors of the fight are they
    And every fight they win."
                    Ring – Ouzel

PELHAM BOOKS/Stephen Greene Press

Published by the Penguin Group
27 Wrights Lane, London W8 5TZ, England
Viking Penguin Inc., 40 West 23rd Street, New York, New York 10010, USA
The Stephen Greene Press, 15 Muzzey Street, Lexington, Massachusetts 02173, USA
Penguin Books Australia Ltd, Ringwood, Victoria, Australia
Penguin Books Canada Ltd, 2801 John Street, Markham, Ontario, Canada L3R 1B4
Penguin Books (NZ) Ltd, 182–190 Wairau Road, Auckland 10, New Zealand

Penguin Books Ltd, Registered Offices: Harmondsworth, Middlesex, England

First published 1975   Revised Edition 1980
Reprinted 1984, 1986   Second Revised Edition 1990

Copyright © 1975, 1980 and 1990 by Mona Huxham

All rights reserved. Without limiting the rights under copyright reserved
above, no part of this publication may be reproduced, stored
in or introduced into a retrieval system, or transmitted in any form
or by any means (electronic, mechanical, photocopying, recording or
otherwise), without the prior written permission of both the
copyright owner and the above publisher of this book.

Made and printed in Great Britain by Butler & Tanner Ltd, Frome and London
Typeset by Granada Typesetting

A CIP catalogue for this book is available from the British Library

ISBN 0 7207 1844 9

Frontispiece: The Reverend John Russell, Vicar of Symbridge 1832–1880.

Contents

Acknowledgements

I am greatly honoured that Her Majesty The Queen, through her Press Secretary, has granted me permission to reproduce a photograph of the painting of Trump which hangs in the harness room at Sandringham.

The Kennel Club were of great assistance in lending me a copy of a photograph they owned to save taking photographers up to Sandringham and I am very grateful to them for trusting me with it. I would also like to thank Mr Augustus Baker and Mr M. Sinnatt CB Senior Executive and Secretary of the Kennel Club for his general interest and help and also the staff of the library of the Kennel Club for all their information and help.

Thanks are given to those who have allowed me to quote from the following: *Jimmy: The Dog in My Life* by Sir Arthur Bryant; *Whose Dog Are You?* by Michael Chance; *British Dogs* by Hugh Dalziel; correspondence from *The Field* and the Jack Russell 'standard' from *Dogs in Britain* by Clifford Hubbard.

I can't begin to thank Miss Una Bremner of Alton who has done the work of reproducing the photograph of Trump and some of the other photographs in this book; Mrs van der Noot for permission to photograph her divine puppies, and Mr Ted Adsett for his very informed descriptions of the breed and permission to reproduce the picture of Dapper. I would also like to thank my daughters: Caroline who did the line drawings and Elizabeth who photographed Mrs van der Noot's puppies.

I am very grateful to Count and Countess Guy de Pelet for their kindness in making Miss Augustus Guests' Pedigrees and letters written by the Reverend John Russell available to me, and to Sir Geoffrey and Lady Howe for lending me the charming photographs of their own Jack Russells taken by John Manners of *The Times*. My thanks also to Sheila Atter for her photographs of Parson Jack Russell Terriers.

Finally I should like to thank the members of the Parson Jack Russell Club for their permission to reproduce their Standard and registration form and typical photographs.

Photo credits
Most of the photographs in this book have been provided by the author but the publishers would also like to thank the following: H.M. The Queen, Carlisle, Sally Anne Thompson, *The Field*, Sheila M. Atter, Ian Johnson, Elizabeth Osman, John Manners, Joe Copping, Mrs Julie Edwards.

Author's Note

When the Rev. John Russell's Centenary was held in April 1983 I was very honoured to be invited to attend. The ceremony was very touching and very well attended and I was able to examine closely the reredos screen that John Russell had had carved by a superb craftsman and which still commands attention in the very beautiful church that John Russell spent so much time and money installing. In the old school room behind the church the Centenary Committee had collected an excellent and interesting amount of memorabilia and I was very pleased to see sections of this book blown up and placed high on the walls around the room for all to see. I sat in those horrible chairs. His favourite portrait of his wife, Penelope, in hunting dress on her mare, was given pride of place. His silver hunting horns, his library of books including Davies' leather-bound biography and all his hunting books and a very important item, the book written for the Rev. John Russell by Edward Capern, *The Chase of the Wild Red Deer*. His hunting top hat, boots and other items were on display and there was a steady line of interested people.

Something that interested me very much were his Church Records and Registers. Every week his signature was on either wedding lines, christening records or funeral details, all done in his own handwriting and over about fifty years his signature is written many hundreds of times.

The following day the local Jack Russell Club held a most enjoyable dog show and afterwards we met in the pub opposite the church which has now been renamed the Jack Russell, where I was persuaded to sign some copies of this book.

At the show I was very pleased to be introduced to Mr Vernon Bartlett who I consider to be the most knowledgeable authority on the original and true Jack Russell Terrier. Mr Bartlett asked me to contact the Kennel Club and to try to see if it would be possible to have the Jack Russell Breed accepted as Kennel Club registered and pedigree dogs. I had already started one rare breed from scratch and for two other breeds' clubs I had been one of the twenty-five founder members, so I agreed to try. It proved harder than I had imagined as most people were happy to stay as they were and felt that the terrier would lose its working quality if bred for show purposes. What we had to do was to form a new club for those people who genuinely wished to be members of the Kennel Club. For my part in the Centenary celebrations I had presented the Jack Russell Club with a framed enlargement of Trump for the Jack Russell who most resembled Trump. Mrs Ruth Wilford won my trophy with her lovely sound Hannah who was very typical. When she rang to thank me I asked her if she would care to join us as I had judged Hannah myself and considered her well worth the award and if I could find twenty-five people with equally good terriers we might make a new Club with dogs the Kennel Club would be able to consider as possible registration material.

We got a club together with Mr Barker as our first President and Mrs Ruth Wilford our very proficient Secretary. We were too eager, I think, and applied to the Kennel Club straightaway only to be turned down as the other Jack Russell Clubs took more delegates and we were voted out. It is almost five years since that first refusal and the Club has made steady progress and at my suggestion only register those applicants that are as near to the required 14–14–14 as possible. Some of them are very like Trump and some very like the picture in Clifford Hubbard's famous little handbook.

One of the most important features of this enterprising club is that they put on similar classes to those run by the Kennel Club and a catalogue is produced.

After five years of going to shows and working as hard as ever my Jack Russells haven't lost any of their verve and vivacity and they are in and out of holes and burrows to their hearts' content.

1 The Origin and Early History of the Breed

The British people have earned a reputation for being the most ardent lovers of dogs, and over the centuries there has been no more popular dog on these islands than the terrier. This word 'terrier' comes from the Latin *terra* or French *terre*, both meaning earth. The dogs so named were originated for the purpose of going underground in order to bolt the foxes or badgers that had retreated to their earths or setts, thus escaping from the people hunting them. Therefore, the terriers had to be well-adapted for going to ground – small to medium in size; narrow in order to fit into the narrow passages; very robust as the work was hard; well-muscled so that they could keep up with the hounds, and so on.

One of the earliest references to terriers was a fourteenth-century manuscript quoted by Strutt in his *Sports and Pastimes*, from which he reproduces an engraving showing three men, two with spades, being assisted by a dog to unearth a fox. The third man is blowing a horn. The dog has a long, narrow head, erect ears a long tail and a smooth coat.

Blaine in his *Rural Sports* reproduces this engraving, but inexcusably converts the dog into a Wire-coated White Terrier, with a dark patch over one eye. He not only fraudulently altered the picture itself but also tried to make it seem of even greater antiquity by describing it as 'Saxons bolting a fox.'

Strutt can be relied on far more, and it would seem that his record is the oldest illustration that we in the British Isles can take to be the most likely predecessor of our modern-day Fox Terrier – the dog our ancestors used when needing a dog to dig after foxes. Four hundred years later, the Rev. John Russell was to find the need for the self-same capabilities in his terriers when he was engaged in hunting foxes over his native Devonshire countryside, and so he in turn was to spend the greater part of his life striving to produce a terrier that would go to earth, worry out the foxes, speak to warn the Foxhounds, and drive the fox away from his hole, without damaging him in any way, so that Reynard was able to tear across country and have the strength to keep well ahead of the hounds and so give the hunt followers a good couple of hours of sport. A terrier with a hard mouth and a 'killer' instinct wasn't what was wanted at all, for if the fox was badly damaged or even killed outright, there was an end to any sport.

What material, therefore, did John Russell find available, when, as Master of Foxhounds, he had to show the hunt followers plenty of good sport in the very 'hollow' country he was forced to hunt over? (By 'hollow' is meant that it was riddled with badger setts and fox hollows, and it was impossible for his servant to fill all of them. His terriers were therefore indispensable.)

Dame Juliana Berners, an Abbess of St Albans, wrote her *Boke of St Albans* in 1486 which contained a 'Treatise on Hunting' which mentioned *terours*. This work proved very popular in the fifteenth-century, and was reissued several times.

While the public of those days were being told what dogs they could expect to find in the hunting field, Dr John Caius, the physician-in-chief to Queen Elizabeth I, published in 1570 a complete classification in Latin of dogs of the time. Under the heading of 'Venatici' (dogs serving the pastime of hunting beasts) was listed 'terrarius'. This work was translated into English by Abraham Fleming in 1576. His translation uses the word 'terrars' and he describes them thus:

> Another sort there is which hunteth the Foxe and the Badger or Grey onely whom we call Terrars, because they creepe into the ground, and by that meanes make afrayde, nyppe, and byte the Foxe and Badger. In such sorte that eyther they teare them in peeces with their teeth, beying in the besome of the earth, or else hayle and pull them perforce out of theyre lurking angles, dark dongons and close caves, or at least through conceaved feare, drive them out of theyre hollow harbours, in so muche that they are compelled to prepare speedy flight and being desirous of the next refuge are otherwise taken and intrapped with snayres, and nettes layde over holes to the same purpose. But these be the least in that kynde called Sagax.
>
> Extract from *De Canibus Britannicis*
> by Dr John Caius, 1570.

Dr Caius wrote in Latin but the above translation into English was made by Abraham Fleming. This was printed in 1576, dedicated to the Dean of Ely, Richard Johnes and sold against St Sepulchre's Church without Newgate. In 1886 a Mr L.U.Gill of 170, The Strand, London reprinted the rare volume in modern form, which is probably the reason this particular treatise on English Dogs is so often quoted. Even so no book on terriers is complete without it. Gervase Markham was a prolific writer who in 1600 wrote about terriers in particular and nearly every other subject of interest as well.

In 1667 Nicholas Cox in his well-known volume *The Gentlemen's*

Recreation tells us that there were in his day two sorts of terriers, one with legs more or less crooked with short coats; the other straighter on their legs and with long jackets. The former could have been the terriers used as 'turnspits' i.e. little dogs that moved in a wheel which in turn rotated the spit on which meat was cooked; the shaggy haired ones were said to be the best workers because they could both chase their prey above ground and drive it from its earth as occasion required. The famous dog author Hugh Dalziel maintained that Cox copied this assertion from early French writers such as de Fouilloux, Stevens and Liebault who were all doctors and contemporaries of Dr Caius, who unfortunately was not a sportsman. Turberville, Surflet and Goodye were physicians who translated Dr Stevens' work from the French of his *Maison Rustique*. Taking the description of the terrier of that date as given by Surflet and Turberville one can see that they were both referring to the same dog but had not copied from one another. The following extract by Turberville out of his *The Noble Art of Venerie and Hunting* is said to have been translated and quoted for all 'Noblemen and Gentlemen' out of the Best Approved Authors which have written about the same:

> Now to speak of the Foxhounds and Terriers and how you are to enter to take the foxe, the badgere and such like vermin: You must understand that there are two sorts of Terriers whereof wee hold opinion that one sort came out of Flanders or the Low Countries as Artoyes and thereabouts and they have crooked legges, and are short-heared most commonly. Another sorte there is which are shagged and streight legged: those with the crokked legges will take earth better than the other and are better for the Badgered bycause they will lye longer at a vermin: but the other with streight legges do serve for two purposes for they wyll hunt above grounde as well as other houndes and enter the earth with more furie than the others but they will not abide so long bycause they are too eager in fight and so come out to take the ayre so there are both badde and good of both sortes.

Quoting immediately from Richard Surflet so that both descriptions can be compared:

> Two Sorts of Earth Dogs. – The hunting of the foxe and brocke, to bee performed with Earth Dogs which are of two sorts: the one hath crooked legs and commonly short-haired: the other hath straight legs and a shagd hair like Water Spaniels: those which have the crooked legs creepe more easilie into the earth than the others and they are best fir the broks, because they stay long there

and keppe better without coming forth. Those which have straight legs serve for two uses, bicause they run as coursing dogs above ground and also take the earth more boldly than the other, but they tarrie not in so long bicause they vexe themselves in fighting with the foxes and brocks bicause they vexe themselves whereby they are forced to come foorth to take the aire.

Blome writing in 1686 in his own *Gentlemen's Recreation* has his own ideas on Fox Terriers and how to put them to work:

The fox is taken with Hounds, Greyhounds, Terriers, etc and that of Terriers there are two sorts. The one is crooked-legged and short-haired and these will take the earth and lye long for either Fox or Badger. The other sort is shagged and straight-legged and these will only hunt above ground as other Hounds but also enter the earth with more courage than the former: but cannot continue there long by reason of their eagerness to pursue the game.

Very honestly Blome admits that he got his information from a French author who is reputed to be the best on that subject in any language. About hunting with Terriers he says further:

As concerning Terriers everyone that is a fox-hunter is of the opinion that he hath a good breed; and some will say that the Terrier is of a peculiar species of itself. I shall not say anything as to the affirmative or negative point. Only give me leave to say that such Terriers as are bred out of a Beagle and a Mastiff generally prove good; for he hath courage and a thick skin as participating of the Cur, and is mouthed from the Beagle.

In further writing of the Terrier Blome says:

This is a very small Dog used for hunting the Fox and Badger: his business being to go into their Earths and to Bay at them – that is to keep them in an angle (a Fox's Earth having divers) whilst they are dug out: for by their Baying and Barking 'tis known whereabouts the Fox is, that he may be the better dug out; and for this use the Terrier is very serviceable being of an admirable Scent to find out. They commonly keep a couple of Terriers to the end they may put in a fresh one to relieve the first.

The above may have been how the French believed the terriers had been obtained but in England, even if some breeders copied Blome and did his amazing cross-breeding there was enough terrier blood in these isles to make such far-fetched sounding methods quite unnecessary. William the Conqueror's wife, Matilda, wove terriers into the Bayeux Tapestry when she showed King Harold hunting with some. Writers have believed that Oppian of Roman times was referring to a 'Beagle' but Clifford Hubbard suggests that we read Terrier instead of Beagle when comparing the translation of Whitaker with that of Dr Henry's *History of England*:

> There is a kind of dog of mighty fame
> For hunting worthy of fairer frame
> By painted Britons brave in war they're bred
> Are Beagles called and to the chase are led
> Their bodies small and of so mean a shape
> You's think them curs that under tables gape.

The word Oppian uses is 'Agassaeus' and the following prose translation also from Oppian may be interpreted as a Beagle or a Terrier as the subject of it:

> Among the noble kinds of dogs that are used for hunting let me note those whose breeds have been sedulously preserved. Thus we see that in Britain there have been specially cherished those dogs that have been termed 'Agassaeus'. All these are adapted by their form to search for their adversaries even in their own burrows for which their apparently feeble aspect does not unfit them. Their gliding motions, their feeble loins, their *wire-like* hair fit them for this purpose and we are enabled to see that their powerful jaws belie the impression of their feebleness. From their aspect it would seem that such impression is not warranted when we see their achievement within the burrows. This breed is especially called the Agassaeus.

Reading all this immediately after the words of Turberville, Surflet and Blome it is easy to suppose that the ancients were mistaken in taking this description to mean a Beagle – it is so exactly right for a Terrier.

In 1707, the Swedish naturalist Carl Linnaeus was born. He made a classification of animals and went into much detail about the different breeds of dogs but, unfortunately, made no mention of terriers. His nearest reference to a terrier breed was 'the Hairy Maltese Dog' which he described as a comforter rather than a worker.

The most outstanding work in this field was written by the Frenchman Georges Buffon, who was also born in 1707. He spent a large part of his life formulating a genealogical tree of all the known races of dogs. He again makes no mention of the terrier as such, so we may assume that the race as known in Britian was not known in France.

In 1718 Giles Jacobs, a writer on legal matters published *The Complete Sportman* which he dedicated to Sir Charles Keymis Bart., of Cefn Mably in the county of Glamorgan (this was the next village to St Mellons where I lived when I was first married – M.H.). Of fox-hunting this book says: 'The fox is taken either with Hounds, Greyhounds or Terriers, etc.,' and then continues in much the same way as most of the other writers I have just been quoting.

It is necessary to generalise on terriers before studying the particular background of the strain of very special ones founded nearly two hundred years ago by the Rev. John Russell and now called familiarly Jack Russell Terriers.

Going back to the earliest beginnings, there always seems to have been in this country a rough-coated, nondescript kind of dog that had a fondness for digging and going down bolt holes and standing up bravely to foxes, badgers and other animals. Their special usefulness was soon apparent and every district eventually achieved a collection of what later became known as terriers because of the nature of their special characteristics. As time went on, they cultivated special attributes according to the nature of the terrain they found themselves in. For instance, the Cairns and Scottish Terriers would be capable of hunting in 'hollow country' which is hunting parlance for rocky ground such as the cairns of the Highlands in Scotland. For this purpose, they

An ancestor of the present day terrier. Such a black and tan terrier had all the necessary attributes but the hounds confused it with the fox with disastrous results.

needed to be very tough, rough-coated to keep them warm and give them added protection against the very rough, stony country they had to work over. Their colours were grey or brindled and black so they couldn't be seen easily by their prey.

The lower and milder climes of the Lowlands and Border country produced the Border Terrier – neat-coated but still rough, with longer legs to cover the ground better in the open country. There can be no doubt that this breed is very well designed for the work he has to do and he is certainly an excellent terrier for the hunts.

Manchester devised the smooth black-and-tan terrier. It is not surprising, knowing the heavy rainfall Lancashire is reputed to have, that the terrier they like best is smooth-coated and so easier to dry and less likely to be weighted down with the mud that would restrict a longer haired breed when going to earth.

As time went on, the number of different terrier breeds sorted themselves out and we find Airedales, Welsh Terriers, West Highland Whites (soon very popular in Scotland as they were easier to distinguish than most of their other breeds who were apt to merge into the countryside too well), Skyes, Dandie Dinmonts, Lakelands, Bedlingtons and so on. There were a great many that were produced purely for sport and never entered into the *Stud Book* of the Kennel Club. Ireland too had Irish Terriers, Kerry Blue Terriers and Glen of Immal Terriers as native breeds – short-haired hard-coated ones and the longer-haired shorter-legged kind to enable them to cover the different kinds of countryside.

Propinquity and knowing the best bloodlines for these very essential hunting qualities caused selective breeding and this soon evolved a special type in a certain district. Once a breed started to emerge, few people would consider introducing a completely 'foreign' bloodline unless this particular bloodline had some extra quality otherwise lacking in the strain. Breeders are often not adventurous enough to venture outside the confines of their known circle of breeding stock. This may be due to ignorance or to the wise axiom that 'the devil you know is better than the devil you don't know.'

John Russell was born at Dartmouth in 1795, and grew up in North Devon, which district was already renowned for its working terriers. He therefore grew up with a knowledge of terriers and it is said of him that he loved country pursuits above all others and spent his boyhood out on the moors with his ponies and dogs. When he was fourteen, he was at Blundells School – still a famous public school in Devonshire – and was severely flogged for keeping ferrets there!

He grew up 'with an eye for a terrier' and all through his fourteen terms at Oxford, where he had to try very hard to get his degree as he spent too much time hunting, he was on the look out for possible dogs.

He would much rather have been studying Beckford's *Thoughts on Hunting* (published in 1798) than the Horace he needed for his finals. Peter Beckford was a hunting squire of repute who had his own pack of hounds that he had bred specifically for the country over which they hunted. He held strong views about terriers too and no doubt his writing had some influence on John Russell when he was forming his own ideas about what was required.

Beckford writes: 'You should always keep a terrier in at the fox; for if you do not he not only may move but always in loose ground may take himself further in. Your country requires a young terrier. I should prefer a black or white terrier; some there are so like a fox that awkward people frequently mistake one for the other. If you like terriers to run with your pack, large ones at times are useful but in an earth they do little good as they cannot always get up to the fox.'

W. B. Daniels, the sporting parson writing some years later, repeated these requirements almost verbatim, but added the following: 'No species of dogs will fight the badger so resolutely and fairly as the terriers of which there are two kinds – the one is rough, short-legged, long-backed, very strong and most commonly of a black or yellowish colour mixed with white; the other is smooth-haired and beautifully formed, having a shorter body and more sprightly appearance, is generally of a reddish brown colour or black with tanned legs; both these sorts are the determined foe of all the vermin kind.' This quotation is taken from Daniels' *Rural Sports*, published in 1801.

These descriptions were all of terriers used against the fox but were not what are called Fox Terriers at the present time. To overcome the colour resemblance to a fox, it can be seen how sensible Masters of Foxhounds would need to concentrate on producing a terrier that was predominantly white with only a few coloured markings. To this end, some used the white terrier with regrettable results because of their temperaments, and some used the Beagle and produced excellent temperaments but Beagles had completely the wrong shape of ears for a terrier. Ears need to be neat, high set and carried dropped forward. The reasons for this are that ears which are too long get caught up in brambles and in the burrows, get in the terrier's eyes, give him a lot of trouble while working and, in any case, the small V-shaped ear with flaps folded neatly over are so characteristic of the terrier and help his alert hearing in no small degree.

All the early writers on dogs are agreed that Sydenham Edwards, who published his *Cynographia Britannica* in 1800 makes a very valuable contibution to the subject of terriers and his subject has obviously been studied at first hand viz:

The Terrier: So called from earthing or entering holes either fox of badger. From the evidence of Oppian's poems he appears to be an original native of this land. Linnaeus says it was introduced upon the Continent so late as the reign of Frederic I. It is doubtless the Vertagus or Tumbler of Raii and others. Raii says it used stratagem in taking its prey some say tumbling and playing till it came near enough to seize.

The most distinct varieties are the crooked-legged and straight-legged; their colour generally black and tanned legs and sometimes reddish-fallow or white and pied. The white kind have been in request of late years. The ears are short, some erect, some pendulous; these and part of the tail are usually cut off; some rough and some smooth-haired. Many sportsmen prefer the wire-haired supposing them harder biters; but experience shows that this is not always the case. Much of the variety of the terrier arises from his being a small dog and often bred for mere fancy.

The terrier is querulous and irascible, high-spirited and alert when brought into action; if he has not unsubdued perseverance like the Bulldog he has rapidity of attack, managed with an art and sustained with spirit; it is not what he will bear but what he will inflict. His bite carries death; he dashes into the hole drives the fox and reluctant stubborn badger into light. As his courage is great so is his genius extensive; he will trace with the Foxhounds, hunt with the Beagle find for the Greyhound, or beat with the Spaniel. Of wild cat, martens, polecats, weasles and rats he is the vigilant and determined enemy; he drives the otter from the rocky clefts on the banks of the rivers, nor declines this combat in a new element.

The picture of the Fox Terrier, 1806 illustrates this point admirably. Obviously to perform all the deeds attributed to him the terrier so described would have to have been a much larger and more powerful species than Fox Terriers or working terriers of the present day. The gameness, pluck and gay abandon is very descriptive of our present day challenger. Badgers and otters aren't hunted now – the badger being protected and the otter is now a rare species and is so much more likely to be preserved than hunted. Still all the above virtues are of a very high order when imbued in the background of today's little hunt terriers and the like and one of which John Russell was only too well aware and was very ready to mould to his liking.

With the advent of fox-hunting in the eighteenth century as well as hunting the hare, the nature of the terrier needed changing dramatically. What was needed then was a faster, sturdy, smaller type that did not punish its prey so much but played with it more and sent it out of its underground den; in the case of hare to chase them out of the

Trump – Parson Jack Russell's first terrier. She was bought from a milkman during his student days in Oxford in 1815. She was the founder of his strain of Jack Russell Fox Terriers.

hedgerows into the open so that the hounds could chase them over the country.

Although in his days as Master of the Hunt John Russell kept his terriers in at the fox only, in his schooldays he often had use for a terrier. He and some of his friends at Blundells School in Devonshire had an understanding with local farmers that they would keep their land free of foxes and other vermin and in return the farmers and the local blacksmith took care of the small pack of hounds that Russell and his friends had collected together. A terrier that would work with the ferrets, help catch rabbits, rats and other vermin was more in line with those schoolboys' requirements, so from quite an early age John Russell had a very strong and personal interest in terriers.

By the time John Russell was in his university days his passion for fox-hunting was well established and one day in 1815 he was punting across the Cherwell with Horace in hand planning to find a quiet spot and pursue his studies in view of the close proximity of his finals, although he would much rather have been studying Beckford, when he met a milkman with just the sort of terrier bitch he had always dreamed of. He refused to budge until he had secured this bitch for his own and this was 'Trump' who was to be the progenitor of the famous race of terriers that he was to become famous for. A picture of Trump on this page shows that she had been docked and her ears had been cropped. Jack Russell was to say that this is the first and last time he ever owned a terrier so mutilated; he much preferred to be able to get his hand around the tail so that when one went to ground he was able to draw it out easily without having to pull it out by its hindleg and possibly damaging his back.

From the picture by Rainagle which was engraved by Scott for the *Sportsman's Cabinet* published in 1803/4 one can see three terriers one of which is white with marks on his head with a patch on the set of its tail. This is a wire-haired dog with a docked tail and erect ears showing traces of a bull-terrier cross from the shape of his head. Another white dog is disappearing down an earth while the third appears to be a dark-coloured dog with a broad white collar, white on muzzle and cut ears. The *Sportsman's Cabinet* tells us that a white pied bitch just like the one in Rainagle's picture gave birth to seven puppies in one litter that were sold at the Running Horse Livery Stable in Piccadilly for 21 guineas – a high price at that period.

T. H. Scott in the *Sportsman's Repository* in 1820 says that the Fox Terrier was not a modern dog for those times but he says history shows that they were evidenced right back to the first century. Scott says there were as good dogs 50 years before and for proof he gives Trump as an example, who was about as perfect point for point as one could hope for.

John Russell was a keen student of Beckford and he wanted his terriers to go after foxes only. However young they were started they were used solely for fox-hunting. He took Trump to Devonshire and mated her to the best of the local terriers and scarcely ever went further afield in his breeding policy in the early days until the time when a good many of the foremost hunts up and down the country started turning out very smart, typical, game, strong and intelligent terriers of white colour only with just a small amount of tan, black and tan or black. These were least likely to be mistaken for a fox during the excitement of a chase and devoured by the hounds. These terriers were bred entirely for work and not for ornament. They would have long open coats, coats of the wrong texture and whereas for show purposes such a coat would have been plucked and stripped to make as neat a picture as possible to catch the judge's eye, no such artifice was practised on the worker. Trump, however looked as neat as a new pin, her lines were splendid, her form absolutley balanced, her outlook keen and stylish. She could have filled the eye of any judge 70 years later, except for her cut ears, as she complied so exactly with the Fox Terrier Breed Standard that was not to come into use for more than 50 years after Trump went to live with John Russell.

In the light of hindsight it must be obvious that Parson John Russell's one aim in his long and full breeding life was to breed a FOX TERRIER par excellence. Basing his ideal on Trump for a pattern we can see when we examine the picture of him with five of his terriers in his study at Tordown or in the frontispiece that he did manage to acquire a race of terriers, as like as peas in a pod. As the background to a breed they were as good or better than any other of the antecedants of any of the top dogs in the breed. The Rev. John Russell was a breeder of Fox Terriers not so-called Jack Russell Terriers. He wouldn't have given house room to those short-legged, bow-fronted, cow-hocked Sealyham cum Corgi crosses that are very often inflicted on the buying public as 'Jack Russell Terriers' – if a pup's parents were 'The best to Ground in the District' as some adverts would have us believe, it still doesn't make it a Jack Russell. Jack Russell's Terriers were 15 to 16 inches at the shoulders and weighed 16 to 18 pounds. They were short-coupled not long backed, neckless wonders his imitators have the audacity to label with his highly respected and much esteemed name. Some detractors of the parson like to suggest that he was nothing more than a dealer and bought and sold any old terrier just to make the odd shilling. This, of course, is absolute nonsense as he needed his terriers every day of his hunting life – and at three hunts a week they were kept very busy. No doubt with his good 'eye' for a terrier he could pick out a good one and from his correspondence people wanted his terriers as far north as Scotland and Ireland too. Having trained his own pack so that they knew every movement of his hand and every sound of his horn he would naturally be reluctant to part with any of them so if he wanted to provide terriers as gifts to his friends, he would have to obtain them somewhere. If Captain Percival Williams, the Master of the Fourbarrow Hounds had looked further he would probably have found that John Russell always got terriers from his grandfather because he found that they were reliable and the type that he liked. The same could possibly have been said of the ones Lord Poltimore remembered Russell got from his father-in-law Gerald Lascelles who was Deputy Surveyor of the New Forest. There were several strains of excellent Fox Terriers in the New Forest at that time viz – the

Left to right Sunday, Push, Sugar, Sputnik – hunt terriers belonging to Captain Percival Williams, M.F.H. the Fourbarrow Hounds. This breed of terrier has been in the Williams family for well over a century and Jack Russell used to buy terriers from them. Note the undocked tails.

Brockenhurst Kennels of Mr H. Gibson and Mr H. M. Maynard's. Mr Gibson bought his first terrier when he was a boy at school about 30 years before the Fox Terrier Club came into being. The baker brought a little terrier bitch when he was delivering bread to the school. He had got her from the gamekeeper at Hams Hall called Massey who had been told to get rid of her as she had killed the favourite cat of the owner of the Hall's mother. Gibson asked to buy it and gave the baker every penny he had in his pockets and the little bitch Fly became the foundation for the famous Brockenhurst Terriers some of the pedigrees of which are included in this book.

Writing about this, 'Stonehenge' in 1879 expressed the view that Beagle blood had been introduced into the Fox Terrier and the breed had become so popular with the public that he was contemptuous about it. 'For the last ten years this pretty little dog has been the favourite companion of Young England and has lately shared the favours of the other sex with the collie, dachshund and the black poodle.' This was very unfair to a sporting dog that managed to retain his sporting instincts whether running with a pack of hounds or simply acting as a companion.

It can be truly said that the Jack Russell Terrier was founded upon several strains of terriers which belonged to the various hunts. They were given names like Old Jock, Old Trap, Old Foiler, Old Buffer and Belvoir Joe. Old Trap was sired by a black-and-tan dog. Possibly Belvoir Joe had the biggest influence on the modern terrier for the name of his son, Belgrave Jack, is to be found in a considerable number of later pedigrees. Old Foiler's dam, Judy, was bred by Parson Jack Russell so it can be seen that, even if he only set out to breed working dogs, the value of his work was appreciated by the show Fox Terrier breeders who came afterwards.

The Kennel Club invited the Rev. John Russell to judge Fox Terriers at the Crystal Palace in 1875 and so it can be seen that he was not 'against' show dogs as such, as some present-day adherents of his would have us believe.

He was a Founder Member of the Kennel Club, whose founder Mr S. E. Shirley was Chairman from its inception in 1873 until 1899, and President until 1904. The Parson was a personal friend and he gave one of his bitches, Pussy, to a Mr Wootton who was a very noted Fox Terrier breeder in the earliest days of the breed as a show dog. Later Mr Shirley obtained Pussy from Mr Wootton for the sum of £40 and the dog joined his not inconsiderable kennel at Ettington Park, Stratford-on-Avon. Mr Shirley was an M.P. and a very keen supporter of the Fox Terrier. He is said to have been delighted with the acquisition of Pussy as we are told that the Parson was always reluctant to let one of his favourites pass out of his possession.

(above left)
Mr A. H. Clarke's champion Result; sire of Venio and Vesuvienne.

(above right)
Bramble (left) and Topper (right) typical hunt terriers of the Jack Russell type. Topper won at Crystal Palace in 1881.

Mr Shirley had a dog, Pantaloon, entered in the first *Stud Book* of the Kennel Club. He had won at Oswestry, Boston and Wellington where he had won cups as well as first prizes. Pantaloon was number 570 in the first edition of the *Stud Book*. His father, Chance II, was by Gammon's Chance out of Nettle by Old Trap. Gammon's Chance was by Tyrant out of Lady; Lady was by Lord Galway's dog out of Cressy's bitch which was bred by the Duke of Rutland who owned the most famous pack of foxhounds in the country – the Belvoir. Tyrant's sire was Old Trap and his dam, Violet, was by Old Jock out of White Violet.

Dame Fortune (left) and D'Orsay (right) were show Fox Terriers from working stock in the 1890's.

Old Trap deserves a paragraph to himself. His pedigree is unknown but he won second prize in Birmingham in 1862. He was white with a tan head and a black spot on one side. The entry in the *Stud Book* ends with '(dead)': I assume that the brackets mean the dog was not alive when the *Stud Book* was printed.

Old Trap was purchased by Mr Bayley from Mr Cockayne, then kennelman to the Oakley Hounds, then at the Tickham Kennels. He was said by Mr Isted to have been sired by a black-and-tan dog. He left Ickwell House, near Biggleswade in Bedford, and went to a Mr Cropper, and afterwards was bought by Mr J. H. Murchison, F.R.G.S., of Surbiton in Surrey, who was said at one time to have had two hundred dogs in his kennel. Old Trap was said to have been bred by Colonel Arkwright, master of the Oakley Hounds, but he was, in fact, bred by the colonel's coachman who took a bitch to a dog called Tip, belonging to Mr Hitchcock, a miller in the area where they lived. This dog Tip was renowned for his great gameness and typical terrier character and he was extensively used in the neighbourhood. The result of this mating was Trap or Old Trap as the foundation of a line was usually referred to. He weighed about 17lb. and he excelled in strength of jaw with a keen eye and expression. His chief faults from a beauty point of view were a slightly long body and cow hocks – both faults that the Parson Jack Russell would detest as good conformation is essential for following the fox. Be that as it may, he was beaten into second place in Birmingham by Old Jock, so we can assume that Jock had the edge on looks.

Old Jock was born in 1859 and bred by Jack Morgan who was Huntsman for the Grove, but the Kennel Club *Stud Book* gives the Master, Captain Percy Williams, equal billing. Old Jock was white with tan on the ears and black at the root of the tail; he also had '(dead)' written next to his entry in the *Stud Book*. His sire was Captain Williams's Jock and his dam was Grove Pepper. It has been said that credit must go to the Grove Hunt for producing this pillar of the breed and the foundation on which many working strains and show models have been built. Old Jock was a biggish dog, 18lb. or so, a trifle thick in the skull but with plenty of jaw power. His bone was ample and he possessed good straight legs and excellent feet. His hindquarters were splendid and all round he was a most symmetrical terrier. He was a show dog and a sportsman as he ran at least two seasons with the Grove hounds. Russell used this dog as a sire.

Old Jock, as the first dog of an important line was referred to in all the stud books, was purchased by Mr Murchison. When he died Jock went to Mr T. Wootton for his weight in silver. Rawdon Lee in the monograph *The Fox Terrier* tells us that John Russell had two of Mr Wootton's stud dogs staying at his home in order to mate them to his

Two very important show winners who were also noted workers. Trimmer (left) sired Belvoir Joe who sired Belgrave Joe. Bellona (right) won the champion prize at Crystal Palace in 1871.

own bitches. Old Jock and Old Tartar were the ones he used and the letter he wrote to their owner about them is most revealing:

I have put one bitch to Jock and shall put another – although she is only nine months old – a rather precocious young lady you will say – tomorrow or the next day; Lord Portsmouth's huntsman will send him on Saturday. I have this bitch – she is seven years old and of my purest blood, and I hope she may not miss.

I never saw a sweeter animal than Jock, so perfect in shape, so much quality. He is as near perfection as we poor mortals are ever allowed to feast our eyes on. His temper is so beautiful and his pluck undeniable, for I had to choke him off a fox. You will naturally ask how I came to know about his pluck and I will tell you. Since they came here I have kept Tartar and Jock chained up in two separate loose boxes because they are warmer than the kennels. Yesterday morning I gave Jock a run before I went to meet the hounds and after my return from hunting I did the same office for Tartar. He went with me very kindly as he had very frequently done before; indeed they both recognised my voice and were mad to come to me whenever they heard it; when suddenly without the least provocation he started back and ran full tilt back to the stable door which was open and in a moment fastened his teeth into Jock. I caught hold of him at once, put his foot in my mouth and bit it with all my force, choking him with my left hand at the same time. Very little harm would have happened had not Jock resented and had him across the nose. When I got Jock's foreleg free Tartar seized his hindleg. I got Jock free and took him in my arms and Tartar fastened on my servant and bit him.

Direct descendants of Old Jock were Olive (left) who lived to be 20 and who won at Crystal Palace in 1881 and at Alexandra Palace in 1882 and Bitters (right).

The whole thing has annoyed me dreadfully and I am sure you will believe jealousy is the cause of the mischief.

Drastic methods for drastic happenings. Anyone in the show world will readily understand John Russell's excitement over the many qualities of Jock. This wasn't the rapture of someone only interested in his working capabilities. John Russell was delighted with his conformation and of course he was looking for this beauty to be transmitted because he had mated Jock to one of his best bitches 'Of his purest blood' as he so proudly puts it. Jock was white with a tan mark on one ear, a black spot at the root of his tail. He stood about 16″ and weighed 18lb. Although all his breeding life John Russell was to put gameness at the top of his requirements for his breeding policy rather than weighing and measuring he nonetheless entered his dogs at the Bath and West Agricultural Show when it was held at Exeter in 1863. It teemed with rain, the building which held the dogs was leaking badly and the poor creatures shivered with cold and misery. The Terrier Classes were judged by a Mr Blyth from London and he put the Hon. Mark Rolle's dogs first and third and the Rev. Russell was placed second.

The following month there was a dog show at Bideford in North Devon and the Rev. John Russell was the judge. The weather was brilliant, there was an entry of 130 dogs and the terriers were divided into three classes – one for smooth-haired dogs, one for smooth-haired bitches and another for rough or wires and then finally one for 'toys'. John Russell was considered an authority on dogs and the *Western Times* gives his qualifications as his knowledge of dogs his love of the *view halloa* and being a good hunter.

After this John Russell was to judge at a great many shows including

Crystal Palace, The Great Yorkshire Horticultural and at the Exeter Horticultural and Dog Show in 1869 where he drew an entry of 335.

In 1868 and 1869 he exhibited at Barnstable and won first prize with a smooth-haired dog named *Fury*. The entries increased each year and dog shows were more and more popular, and from a rather poor start terriers and Fox Terriers in particular were catching on fast. They had risen from the position of assistants to rat-catchers and vermin controllers, risen from the lowly confines of the spit, left the position of aide de camp to all the schoolboys and poachers and the like. Queen Victoria had made dog owning respectable and the Prince and Princess of Wales made dog showing a highly desirable pastime. The Fox Terrier by virtue of his smart looks, keenness, good temperament and adaptability soon enhanced socially and soon everybody that was looking for a breed to show was seriously considering the Fox Terrier. To start with anything that was docked and had black and tan markings was entered at the shows but the prize winners were always the 'Kennel Terriers' from the various hunts, where we have seen that some of them took great pride in their terriers.

Four or five guineas wasn't too much to pay for a handsome, well-bred Fox Terrier – as much as £20 had been paid for an especially desirable specimen and when it is realised that Parson John Russell only earned £180 a year to keep the vicarage, his wife and son, pay several servants, feed his horses, dogs and give generously to all the many charities his kind heart deemed necessary, it will be realised that £20 and even £5 was a lot of money. In the late eighteenth and early nineteenth centuries, Squire Thornton, Mr. Foljambe, my fellow countryman, Sir Watkin Wynn – who the Hampshire squire Gilpin tells us filled his hall in the New Forest with hounds and terriers – and Col. Thornton the Yorkshire squire whose 'Pitch' is the ancestor of many winning terriers, were some of the top breeders. 'Viper' with a heavily marked rather coarse head had the most beautiful shape and was, apart from her head, as good as terriers that came 100 years later. The different countries mentioned had widely differing types of country over which they had to hunt so that individual hunts would have a preference for a terrier that was especially adapted to their particular countryside. Sometimes a Master, just like John Russell had a special fancy for a certain type of terrier and he would concentrate on producing this particular type to the exclusion of all else. Sometimes the quality of the terrier was influenced a great deal by the good or bad features of the local stud terrier or terriers. Before the coming of the railways it was a long and costly business travelling across the land to a special stud dog in order to improve the breeding of one's terriers. Russell frequently visited hunts up and down the country – even as far as Wales, Brecon and Scotland as well as all over his native Devon and

Cornwall all the way to Bodmin Moor, where he hunted regularly. All these parts of the country had terriers with their packs and Russell in his quest for the perfect terrier for his purpose had his choice.

The pity of it is that Parson John Russell's pedigrees and Kennel records have been lost for all my information on the subject leads me to say without hesitation that Jack Russell was breeding a 'Fox Terrier' as such and not some sort of a short-legged, long-backed, mis-shapen corgi or bassett crossed to go to ground sort of type to aid him in his favourite hobby. We know how much he regarded his hounds and chose the very best of their kind always to the very highest standard. It couldn't be considered for a moment that he would look for anything less in his terriers, that had to live with him in the house as his constant companions, than something clean of limb, lithe and active – in fact well able to keep up with his famous hounds and then run 30 or 40 miles home again. Jack Russell is credited with breeding only wires, but what he did have was a 'hard' coat that from the length of a cricket pitch would look smooth. This coat often referred to as 'broken' would give the terrier good protection against cold winds, wet and sharp branches and gorse that they would have to contend with, but *would not* be long enough to get caught up on brambles and such. Clifford Hubbard's picture of a Jack Russell Terrier in the *Observers's Book of the Dog* illustrates this point exactly and breeders as such advertise three kinds of coats for the Jack Russell – smooth, broken and wire-coated. Jack Russell loved and admired 'Old Jock' who was smooth. Remember that he said in describing Jock 'I never saw a sweeter animal than Jock, so perfect in shape, so much quality. He is as near perfection as we poor mortals are ever allowed to feast our eyes on.' Does this sound like a breeder who would put up with the sight of any ugly old terrier just so long as it would drive the fox out of its den? He had much better heads on his own terriers than the one my good friend Clifford Hubbard depicts and showed and won 1st prizes with.

The *Sporting Magazine* of May 1841 – referring of course to John Russell – says:

> The hounds did their work admirably and I have seldom seen a neater pack; they are certainly small for fox-hounds: the greater part of them are black white and tan, not one yellow and white hound amongst them. They are accompanied by a couple of neat terriers; one of them called 'Tipoo' is one of the most perfect dogs in his calling I have ever seen.

The Rev. John Russell was always ready to give advice to younger Masters of Hunt that came after he gave up his pack of hounds in 1870. Among those, the Hon. Mark Rolle was one, whose terrier was put over John Russell's the first time the old man showed his dogs. J. C. Hawker of East Anstey, in Wales and Mr Lawrence the master of the Llangibby Hunt in Wales were special friends and visited regularly. My husband hunted with the Llangibby always as it was his local pack, so we know the sort of country John Russell liked to visit. While staying with Captain Pennell Elmhirst, the Master of the Woodland Pytchley, he mounted John Russell for the first meet of the Quorn that particular season. One thousand or more horsemen turned out and although many came to grief because there were still so many leaves about, John Russell was not among them. The next day Tuesday he was out with the Cottesmore at Tilton Gate and on the Wednesday he was at Croxton Park for a meet of the Belvoir, but this time in a carriage for by this time John Russell was in his 84th year. The day following the meet of the Belvoir Russell visited the kennels of the Duke of Rutland at Belvoir Castle, and the next day went to Bath where he saw the Beaufort meet at the Cross Hands Inn. He arrived back in Devonshire in time to see Lord Portsmouth's hounds and take the service on the Sunday. This does not sound as though the Rev. John Russell was just a 'local' breeder with only the very restricted blood of Devonshire to produce his so famous strain of Fox Terriers that their fame even in the middle of the nineteenth century was spread far beyond these shores. His hounds were bought by German Barons and people of the top escutcheon so why not his terriers who were certainly bred just as carefully – and from the two pictures of them in this book together with the blood of their common ancestor the estimable Trump gave him a very good hand indeed. His wide choice of sires would further aid in his efforts as when he visited any of the famous Hunt Kennels, where he was always welcome for the excellent advice he had at his fingertips, no stud dog of any consequence, anywhere, would have been ignored.

To the end of his long life John Russell was to have his terriers with him, many of them in the house as personal pets and as they passed on great was the old man's grief when he had to say goodbye to a special favourite. When he died, Rags, who had lost an eye in a fight with a cat, Sly, Fuss and Tinker were with him. He gave all his terriers away but they were not always appreciated all that much because he refused to have them docked or their ears cropped, with the result that they could not be used for show purposes.

Idstone, the famous canine author, in his very valued book *The Dog* published in 1872 says that like Parson Jack Russell he likes a small terrier, hating 'lumber' in any sporting animal. He always had a terrier or two about the place, tracing back to Jack Russell's Devonshires, which were well up to his standard or he would not have kept them. The Parson's terriers were always game and hardy – his was a bit too hard in the mouth and he thinks that is why Russell had parted with it.

In looks his terrier was white with blue-black ears, one blacked marked eye, black nose with a smudgy marking on it and he is rather leggy which is no great objection as he had to run and keep up with the hounds, rather narrow in the chest to give speed, as he had never seen a fast animal with a wide chest. His tail disfigures him for me as it it rough and like a brush sticking up. Legs, feet are all right and he has a good neck though he is upright in shoulder which I abhor but the chest is deep and so are the back ribs. Weight about 13lb., face too blunt for beauty but it is covered with hair as short and close as a pointer's. Ears short, thin and close to head, coat rather long, harsh and hard yet perfectly smooth. Legs clean-cut and the whole profile of the dog sharp and defined when set up on his hackles. Idstone was told that his dog was of the pure blood that John Russell had bred for forty years and it was a Fox Terrier. He was, however not too sure that the rather coarse head and rough stern didn't evidence some alien blood being introduced. The Parson, himself was very disparaging of the terriers that were being shown at one of the shows he attended and told his companion that among the one hundred and fifty entries there was hardly a decent Fox Terrier. 'In fact I rarely see a real Fox Terrier', said the Parson, adding:

'They have so intermingled strange blood with the real article that, if he were not informed, it would puzzle Professor Bell himself to discover what race the so-called Fox Terrier belongs to.'

'And how is that managed?' asked his friend adding, 'I can well remember Rubie's and Tom French's Dartmoor terriers and have myself owned some of that sort worth their weight in gold'.

'True *terriers* they were' said Russell, 'but different from the present show dogs as the wild eglantine differs from a garden rose. The process is simply as follows: they begin with a smooth terrier bitch then they mate her to an Italian Greyhound to obtain a *finer skin*. The ears of this cross could be an eyesore to the connoisseur so a beagle is introduced and so little is seen of that defect in the next generation. These two breeds are not noted for their courage so lastly a *bulldog* is introduced to give the necessary fearlessness. The composite animal described above became the foundation of the *modern* fox-terrier. The bulldog blood gave courage, it is true, but far too much of it because the old pit-dog was bred to kill and so would inflict too much punishment on its fox either by killing it outright or badly damaging it so that it can't get away for the hunt to chase it. Secondly hard-mouthed terriers are proper little biters and often fight to the kill down the fox-holes themselves.'

Russell bred some top class show Fox Terriers and Judy or Juddy was one that he registered in the Kennel Club Stud Book. A long line of Juddy's has been traced, which are all smooth coated. One of these was still alive in South Africa in 1957 and came originally from Bath. His owner, Mrs Speding of Kenya, describes him as a typical smooth-haired terrier with the typical black patch near his tail. He had a good length of leg and weighed about 17lb.

Our Dogs of August 1956 printed an article by the judge and breeder Dr Krasilinikoff of Denmark in which he stated that according to their Fox Terriers Club Stud Book No. 1 there were still descendents of some of the old parson's terriers about. 'The ancestress of the Wire Fox Terrier family No. 73 is coming from a bitch of Jack Russell's strain in about 1878. This family is shown in Great Britian. The new champion Graigydan Fearnought is out of that family, so is Mitre Quicksilver who won a challenge certificate at the L.K.A., in 1950. He is a very good show dog, a Danish and Swedish champion as well as a good dog underground. A couple of days ago he went after a fox when we were out walking in a wood and soon he found the place but the fox was not at home. He was very disappointed was my good Slavin. So the modern Wire can still do his work if he has the opportunity. Slavin is by Ch. Travella Strike.'

The difference between the rough and smooth-coated terrier has been accentuated in the last seventy years and the two are now completely different in appearance. H. Compton writing in 1902 says that the wires were not nearly as popular as the smooths before about 1892. Yet the wire was the Reverend John Russell's breed and what does that not imply? For where shall you find any terrier strain or for that matter any strain of dogs so honoured and renowned as that of the Devonshire Parson, whose distaste for show dogs was almost as profound as his admiration for working ones? I suppose he is the only terrier fancier who achieved a world-wide reputation for his stock without the aid of red tickets and championship certificates. Mr Russell has been called the father of the breed; he started his strain in Waterloo Year and he died in 1883 and his experience comprehended the whole gamut of type from the chaotic to the completed. He was as particular about the pedigrees of his own dogs as the most expert and successful of modern exhibitors, and only once admitted an outcross when he imported a dash of old blood from Old Jock. It would surely be new blood for him and what about Old Tartar? We have John Russell's letter to Mr Tom Wootton his friend to whom he gave Pussy, that he used this other dog as well.

There is a lot of evidence that John Russell, towards the end of his life, started to deal in terriers. There is still no evidence that he sold any though, but a lot of people have stated that they had been 'given' terriers by the Parson, and in every case they were delighted with their presents. The only snag was if they wished to show them for John Russell was too kind hearted to have his terriers' ears cut just to make them 'show specimens'. He had a personal theory about the tails too for he left them undocked so that he could get his hand around them when pulling them out of the earths.

In my book by Stonehenge, the editor of *The Field* and the editor of the *Kennel Club Stud Books* in the early days states:

> The Rev. John Russell in the West of England was long famous for his strain of rough terriers, so closely resembling the modern dogs exhibited by Mr Sanderson, Mr Carrick and Mr Lindsay Hogg as to be inseparable by any ordinary test.

These terrier owners kept orthodox terriers which conformed to the Kennel Club standards and many of their animals had successful careers on the bench. It can be seen from this that Russell's terriers were perfectly good specimens of the breed of Fox Terriers as far as conformation and type were concerned. The Kennel Club had not been thought of when John Russell started his strain. When it was started by his personal friend Mr S. E. Shirley in 1873 John Russell had already been breeding his terriers for well on 60 years. He had Judy or Old Juddy as the first in a famous line were apt to be called in those days, entered in the first stud book and his address was given as J. Russell, Barnstaple, Devon.

Russell's terrier blood was to be found in many of the old champions. Mr Carrick of Carlisle was the owner of Carrick Tack that was a great winner and grandson of John Russell's 'Fuss'. Carrick showed these wire-haired terriers and by using Kendal's Old Tip (notice the name) bred some excellent wires, such as his Venture. Mr Shirley also had a Tip by Kendal's Old Tip so did Mr Hayward Field but he changed the name to Tussle.

The wires were said to be much better workers as they had been bred entirely for work. There had been no cross-breeding to improve them for show purposes and so they were much purer than the smooths.

When Parson John Russell judged the Kennel Club Show at the Crystal Palace in 1874 he was 79 years of age and was to die nine years later, so of course he didn't do much judging after that. It wasn't because he did not like show dogs and judging them at all as some of his adherents would have us believe: but rather because he was so very interested in the Fox Terrier – it was his special breed – he had founded his own strain and he loved it as those of us who create things – any work of art, produce a family or bring a garden into being love the object of their creation. What did worry him about 'showdogs' as apart from other Fox Terriers was the fact that owners paid such high prices for their show specimens that they were loath to put them to work in case they got so damaged that they could not be shown – his Rags had lost an eye and badgers often mauled the terriers so badly that they were marked for life. Although he only sent his after foxes they could easily meet up with a badger – a much fiercer animal altogether, and one his terriers, which were on the small side, could have found it too much for them. All his were hand picked for pluck and gameness and would not have hesitated to tackle something beyond their capabilities. They were taught not to bite hard too which would have made them easy prey for a badger.

John Russell delighted in Old Jock and was particularly pleased that he had run two seasons in the hunting field before starting his show career.

John Russell knew what he was about for when he judged Fox Terriers at the Crystal Palace from the 9th to the 12th June 1874 he drew a large proportion of the entry of the all-breeds show which amounted to 1,187 dogs in all the breeds. This show, held under the management of the Kennel Club, had the Rev. Pearce (Idstone) judging Bloodhounds and Mastiff and John Russell also judged Harriers. The following notes are from *The Kennel Club Stud Book No. 2*.

> John Russell made two dogs tie in the Championship Class for Smooth Fox Terriers, namely Mr J. Fletcher's *Rattler* and Mr F. J. Ashbury's *Tyke*. Rattler was by *Fox* out of *Fan* by *Spot* out of *Dutch*. Fox by Trimmer II who was by Old Tartar, one of the stud dogs Russell used on his own breeding. *Old Tartar* No. 592. *Tyke* No. 615 Mr H. Gibson late Mr F. J. Ashbury breeder the Hon. T. W. Fitzwilliam. By Tartar No. 592 out of Carry by Murchison's *Old Jock* No. 558 out of Chester Nettle.
>
> He did the same thing in Bitches for he made Mr J Shepherd's *Lillie* and Mr S. Dixon's *Myrtle* equal first as well. Lillie No. 666 was by *Tartar* No. 592 out of *Patch* No. 635 by *Old Fell's Spot* out of *Daisy* by Bishop's *Bob* out of *Crafty* by *Old Jock* out of Simpson's *Nettle*: *Bob* out of Spencer's bitch from Clifton by Sir R. Clifton's *Trap* out of *Vic*: *Trap* by *Old Jock* out of *Grove Nettle* No. 655 *Myrtle* No.674 bred by Mr Luke Turner by Sale's *Sam* out of *Jenny* by Murchison's *Old Jock* No. 558 out of Page's *Huz*: *Sam* by *Tyrant* out of *Vic* by *Old Jock*.
>
> Open Class –   Dogs 1st Mr H. Gibson's *Rivet*
>   2nd Mr J. Shepherds *Buffett*
>   3rd Mr H. Gibson's *Flasher*
>   4th Messrs H. North, W. Shaw & Co.'s *Merry*

Open Class Bitches   1st Mr H. Gibson's *Spiteful*
2nd Mr C. A. Horsfall's *Giddy*
3rd Mr J. H. Shore's *Fury*

There was a special prize for puppies under twelve months old, dogs and bitches and this was won by Mr H. Gibson's *Bustle*.

Rivet No. 584 (white with evenly marked head by *Gadfly* No. 4113 out of *Tricksey* by *Brock* out of *Lady* by *Newton's Jim* out of *Lady*: *Brock* by *Old Jock* No. 558 out of White's *Venom*.

Buffett by De Castro's *Buffer* out of Frolic by Foiler: *Buffer* No. 524 by *Bounce* out of *Trinket*.

Flasher No. 4110 by Gibson's *Foiler* out of *Brockenhurst Nettle*: by Sale's *Hornet* out of *Cottingham Nettle* by *Old Jock* No. 558 out of *Wasp*.

Bitches

Gibson's *Spiteful* by *Old Sam* out of *Frantic*, by *Foiler* No. 537.

Horsefall's *Giddy* bred by H. Gibson by *Old Grip* out of Hopcraft's *Trap* by *Trap* No. 4139 out of *Vic* by *Tartar*.

Shore's *Fury* No. 645 (white with small spot over left eye) breeder Mr Luke Turner by *Belvoir Joe* out of *Venom* by *Old Rap*. *Belvoir Joe* by Cooper's *Trimmer* out of *Grove Nettle*. *Belvoir Joe* was out of *Trinket* by *Trap* out of *Nettle*.

It is amazing how time and time again he picks out terriers going back to his own favourite Old Jock; sometimes three and four generations after his blood was introduced into a breeding policy.

The various packs of hounds all over the country had several terriers each by the middle of the nineteenth century, but not all of them took any pride in the selection and breeding of these terriers, being content that they were able to keep up with the pack and willing to go to ground to drive out the bolted fox. There were exceptions to this: the Grove, the Oakley, the Belvoir, the Pytchley and the Quorn were some that bred for looks as well as ability in the hunting field. All these hunts were contemporaries of Parson Jack Russell's own pack and he was at the height of his prowess with another twenty years to live when Old Jock was born.

Another of the pillars of the breed was Grove Nettle who was bred in 1862 by W. Merry, Huntsman to the Grove hounds, her sire being Grove Tartar and her dam the Rev. W. Handley's Sting. She is said to have been a very pretty tan-headed bitch with a black patch on her side and a very profuse coat – the first time we have read about a wire in these records. She had a great reputation for work as well as for her looks.

From these three terriers – Old Trap, Old Jock and Grove Nettle – came all that was best in the Fox Terrier breed. As they were all from hunt packs, they left close relations who never got near a show ring but were none the worse for that, and some would continue the good looks of their parents in the hunting field and others would carry some faults into the show ring.

Grove Nettle was a prolific mother and was mated to nearly all the best dogs of her day. She is recorded as having had Nectar from her mating to Old Jock and this line produced the famous Ch. Raffle. Mated to Old Trap, she bred Cooper's Trinket, the dam of Belvoir Joe who in turn sired the all-time great, Belgrave Joe.

The Belvoir Hunt was especially proud of its hunt terriers not only because they had produced a strain of smart lookers, but also for their tremendous keeness for their work. Although they seemed to have kept largely to their own lines, it is probable that they sometimes used the terriers of the Grove Hunt as an outcross and vice versa, because the Morgan family of huntsmen, who were well-known keen Fox Terrier enthusiasts, had members in both hunts in charge of the hounds.

The best one they bred by these means was Belvoir Joe, who has gained immortal fame for being the sire of Belgrave Joe, whose blood is reputed to have been responsible for the show Fox Terrier of today. Some say that Belgrave Joe was bred by Luke Turner of Leicester, but he was actually bred by John Bransom on 31 July 1869 and it was not until he was advanced in years that Mr Turner bought him for £20. He was a great favourite with his new owner and lived to be twenty years old. He was exhibited 'not for competition' but to show breeders what he was like and the description of him by Sidney Castle, who saw him, is as

Sting (left) dam of Grove Nettle and grandmother of Jack Russell's Juddy. Venio (right) was one of the breed's top sires and a winner in 1889 and 1893.

follows:

> I shall never forget his beautiful head, his great character and true keen terrier expression, perfect shoulders and his good legs and feet, although a very old dog. For all-round type and excellence, he was a brilliant example and by having the faculty of transmitting much of his good points to his own sons and daughters, it is little wonder that his blood is so much sought after. Although only used as a sire in his old age, he left us such terriers as Brockenhurst Joe, Olive and Spice whose successful sons and daughters were legion. The skeleton of Belgrave Joe stands under a glass case in the smoking room at the Kennel Club, restored recently by a few of the late Mr Turner's friends, of whom I was proud to be one.

Close inbreeding was followed and Grove Nettle was mated back to her father, Grove Tartar, and this time she produced Grove Willie, the great grandsire of Old Foiler, who was bred in North Devon – not far from the living of John Russell – by a Mr Whitemore of Silverstone. Old Foiler's sire was Old Grip and the dam was Old Judy brother and sister by Grove Willie out of Vixen, who was by Grove Tartar out of his daughter Grove Nettle. Such close breeding as this illustrates would appal present-day breeders, and their vets even more. However, from the picture of Champion Venio, born in 1888, an end product of this breeding with five lots of Old Foiler in the line of the sixth generation, it can be seen that there was a lot to be said for what they did.

Old Foiler was shown in Birmingham in 1874 where he won, and the judge, Mr Gibson of Brockenhurst in Hampshire claimed him for £100. This dog was said to have a good head but a tendency to a drooping

Left: Vesuvienne, full sister to Venio, and a broken-coated descendant of Trump.

Right: The Belgravian was a smooth-coated descendant of Trump. He was exported to M. George Kryn of Holland.

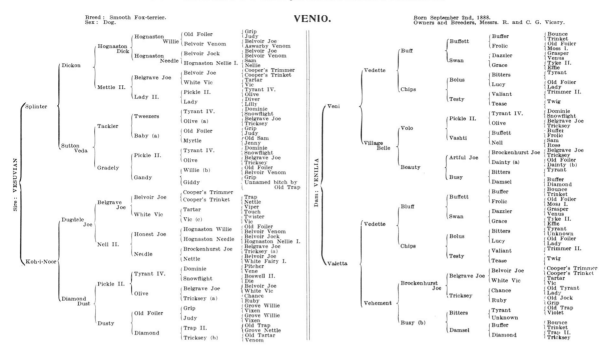

Fig. 1 Pedigree of Venio

hindquarter and double dew claws on his hind legs. These two characteristics are found today, so if it is a problem that troubles breeders, this is probably where it originated.

The Rev. Dr Rosslyn Bruce tells us that John Russell bred Juddy in 1868. Could this have been anything to do with Old Juddy mentioned above, who was by Punch out of Crafty by Twig out of Vic? Punch was by Old Tarquin by Old Jock out of Grove Nettle. Twig is given as being bred by a Mr J. Russell in 1866 by Jock out of Lord Bentinck's Tartar, out of J. Russell's Vic.

We know from his memoirs that Parson Jack hunted with Tip, Nelson and Nettle which he bred, and Hugh Dalziel in his *British Dogs* says: 'The Rev. John Russell, who is certainly the father of the Fox Terrier Breeders, tells us that he has bred his dogs since 1815 and their pedigree has been kept quite pure, except that he once admitted an admixture of Old Jock – a high compliment to the old dog.'

Old Jock and Grove Nettle's daughter, Nectar, was born in 1865 and was bred by a Mr Cropper. She changed hands and in turn was owned by Mr F. Sale, Mr Page and Mr Wootton. She was eventually owned by the Hon. T. W. Fitzwilliam of Wentworth Woodhouse, Rotherham, and is on both sides of the extended pedigree of Brockenhurst Worry.

In 1869, the Hon. Mr Fitzwilliam registered a dog called Trumps,

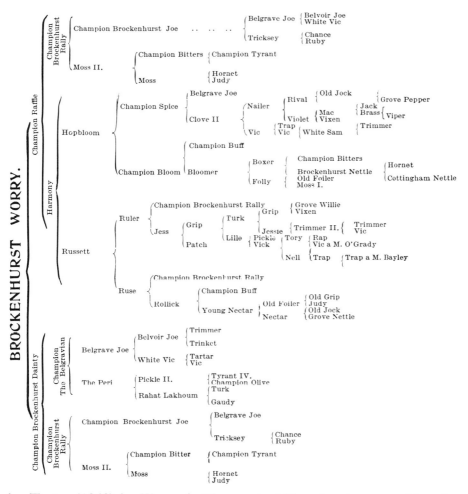

Fig. 2   Pedigree of Brockenhurst Worry

by Tartar (1862) by Weaver's Viper out of Touch, who was said to be wire-coated. Viper was born in 1863 by Hassel's Viper out of Nettle (1863) who was by Young King Dick out of Nettle (wire-coated).

Mr Wootton owned a wire Fox Terrier named Tip who was born in 1872 and bred by Mr G. Sanderson of Cottenham by Kendalls Old Tip of the Sinnington Hounds. He also showed Tip's brother Venture, who was born the year before, and they were both first prize winners at the Crystal Palace.

To take the line a bit further, the Mr Gibson who bought Old Foiler owned a kennel in the New Forest which he made famous by using only the best blood available. Among his many winners were Brockenhurst Joe, Vixen, Bitters, Diamond and the most famous of all, Dorcas, who was born in 1873 and was acclaimed by all who saw her as the best terrier of her time.

All the books that describe Dorcas are agreed that if she were alive today – over a hundred years later – she would make an equally good impression. She was bought by Mr Frederick Burbidge who was the captain of the Surrey County Cricket Eleven for many years. He was the squire of Micklefield, a keen follower of the Old Berkeley Foxhounds, a good shot, first-class fisherman and, in fact, an all-round good sportsman. It would be natural for him to demand a high standard in the dogs he acquired and in Dorcas by Old Foiler, Bloom by Buff and Nettle (again the name being carried down) he had three of the best bitches of the day.

The Surrey Cricket Eleven were not having a very successful period just then and Fred Burbidge achieved two ambitions – 'to see Surrey put cricket at the Oval on its legs again and to breed the best Fox Terriers of all time'. When Surrey became champion county he succeeded in one respect and was well on the way to the other when he collapsed and died and his kennel was dispersed. When the sale of his terriers was completed, the net amount the 'Hunton' strain reached under the hammer was £1,750.

Many good little hunt terriers were recorded in the New Forest and other districts where a lot of show winners were being bred. From an article in the *Fox Terrier Chronicle*, it would appear that the better looking ones were sorted out and easily disposed of to the growing number of people who were being caught in the increasingly popular sport of exhibiting rather than working their dogs. The lead was being given by the Royal Family. Queen Victoria and the Prince Consort, the Prince and Princess of Wales and their family all showed their dogs regularly.

It is easy to see that those kept for working had to possess faults that made them undesirable to prospective show ring buyers and so, when they were bred closely in their own circle, they were inclined to produce stock which had a double share of faults. Therefore, a dog that was too short in the leg to win prizes was kept in the hunt kennel and mated to a bitch that also had been turned down for showing because her legs were too short. The next generation would, therefore, have a preponderance of short legs. As these made excellent workers and had inherited a double dose of all that was good in the Rev. John Russell's and other top class breeders' dogs, they found their own level in the world and have been in demand for the job which they do so well, ever since.

The fact that they all must have faults in order to keep them from being sold for high prices into the show ring, is no doubt the reason why some of the older 'diehards' are so bitterly opposed to them. By and large, they have been a faulty lot but with some exceptions. Now and again a very specially good one emerges. If all the good ones could be collected together and bred from, it is possible that a standard could emerge.

Evidence shows that in Devon, where John Russell established his strain, some very good terriers still exist on the lines he laid down. When John Russell died in 1883, the late Arthur Heinemann bought up every terrier that could trace back to Russell-bred ancestry 1871–1930.

A Henry Scale obtained some dogs from the Parson and he and his son, and later his grand-daughter Joan Begbie, continued the strain. Four of hers were photographed together and very level-looking they are – one smooth and three with rougher looking coats and whiskers. They can be seen in the July 1965 issue of the now discontinued magazine *Family Pets*. They are quite short-legged and Joan Begbie vouches for their authenticity, although adding that the Jack Russell blood from the Parson's line has of necessity been diluted.

During my research for this book, I was constantly coming across letters and articles decrying the smooth-coated terrier and I read how John Russell's grand-daughter is said to have declared that the Parson never had a smooth coat in his house (see page 166). The picture of his study with five of his dogs shows what appear to be smooth-coats. The coat of the Jack Russell Terriers had a very special characteristic because although it looked smooth from a distance, it was actually hard and wiry to protect them against the cold and wet and the rough and stoney ground they had to work with. This picture of his dining-room

Parson Jack Russell's terriers in his dining room at Tordown.

at his Tordown Vicarage shows the chairs which were covered with the hides of his favourite hunters and standing on the said hunters' legs – hooves and all!

From the above, it will be seen that Parson Jack Russell was not alone in his quest for a good sporting terrier to aid his hunting activities. Where he differed was in finding his ideal right at the beginning when he acquired Trump and bred every future litter to her very outstanding pattern.

The year before Belgrave Joe was born, Russell bred a bitch called Judy or Juddy (see page 21) and she is the foundation bitch of the modern smooth Fox Terrier exhibition model, whether his adherents like it or not. She is the direct ancestress in tail female line of champions Travelling Fox, Aire Ideal, Dunsrex Flying Rose Marie and many other outstanding show terriers of modern times.

Three of Russell's dogs were called Tip, Nettle and Nelson. Tip is descended from Trump and was a wizard in the hunting field, having a sort of 'second sight' about what the fox was going to do. Davies tells the story of how on one occasion when the hounds were in close pursuit of a fox they suddenly saw Tip going off at full speed in the opposite direction. It was not long before the fox made for Greys Holts which had been where Tip had gone to. The fox arrived at Greys Holts to find Tip dancing about, throwing his tongue frantically and doing his utmost by noise and gesture to scare the fox away from the nearby earth. Perfect success crowned the manoeuvre. The fox, not daring to face the 'lion' in his path, gave the spot a wide berth while the hounds, carrying a fine head, passed on to the heather and after a thrilling run killed him on the open moor. It was a case of the dog putting two and two together and saying to himself that the fox, who had only been on foot ten minutes, really intended to gain Greys Holts. It was as though the dog had said to himself, 'No, no. You're the same fox that gave us the slip once before but you are not going to play that trick again.'

Tip lived to be a very old dog but he hardly ever missed a day's hunting. Davies tells us that no man on earth could catch him once he had seen Russell with his top boots on.

What is of interest to us reading all this information at the present time, and without the Parson's pedigree records to confirm or deny it, is, was this Tip an ancestor – father or grandfather for instance – of the Tip that was the sire of Old Trap (see page 21)? Did Mr Hitchcock, the miller, obtain him from Parson Jack Russell? There is no doubt at all that he was a dog of very high quality who had earned a reputation for transmitting these qualities to his offspring. He had earned more than would have been expected from just an ordinary dog bought to keep the mill clear of rats. There was something very special about Old Trap and his colour corresponded with that of Trump. It is obvious that

Jack Russell was breeding high-class terriers, not only the 'new ones' so often connected with his name.

The Mr Wootton to whom he gave Pussy was interested in wire-coated terriers. He is noted several times in the *Stud Book* with smooths and at the Fourth Terrier Show, Mr Wootton, acting for Lord Lonsdale, bought the wire-coated terrier Briggs for £200, Miss Nuggs for £105 and Vera for the same price; Sam Weller for £100, Snowball for £100 and Bundle for £42. These very high prices, even by today's inflated standards, for what the smooth-coated Fox Terrier fraternity looked on as 'outcasts', came as a big shock to them. In 1898, at Birmingham Show, a wire-coated terrier Ch. Go Bang did very well and afterwards was sold by Mr George Raper for £500. It was obvious that the wire-haired terrier had arrived, although still very new then, in the show ring.

Parson Jack Russell was an accepted member of this rather exclusive circle — both by upbringing and because of his very sporting ways and love of everything to do with horses and dogs which earned him great popularity.

In 1865 while officiating as a judge at the Royal Agricultural Society's Show at Plymouth, he was invited to dine with the Prince of Wales, later King Edward VII. This started a life-long friendship with the Royal Family and, when the Parson died, the Prince bought the painting of Trump at the sale of his effects. It was placed in the harness room at Sandringham where it hangs to this day.

John Russell married Penelope Bury, daughter of Admiral and Mrs Bury of Dennington House, near Barnstaple, and she shared all his love of country living and pursuits. When the Bishop of Exeter commanded him to give up the Mastership of his pack lest it interfere with his clerical duties, she offered to take it over in his stead.

Their life together, although of great fellowship and contentment, was marred by the loss of their first child, a son, who was born on 29 May 1827, and died only one year later on 31 May 1828.

Parson Jack Russell was ordained in 1819 and became curate of the parish of George Nympton near South Molton in North Devon — not a stone's throw from the home of my husband's grandfather who lived in the parish of Chulmleigh, South Molton, and also hunted the district until the end of a very long life. Russell's stipend was a mere £60 per year, out of which he had to keep his horses and hounds, as well as to maintain his household. At this time, he took up otter hunting and had to reorganise his pack of foxhounds who did not take too well to this new mode of hunting. He bought a hound called Racer from a local farmer and as this hound seemed to lead the rest of the pack, matters improved.

'Russell,' to quote his biographer Davies, 'entered on the work of ministry with a due sense of the sacred office and his own responsibility, which no doubt will be questioned by many who have only heard of his prowess in the hunting field. He made an excellent minister and visited the sick and the poor and was for ever ready to administer consolation all round. He preached God's word with fervour and would visit any neighbouring pulpit whenever invited to do so. He even preached at Sandringham Church having been commanded to "put a sermon in his pocket" when visiting the Prince and Princess of Wales.'

He was delighted to become curate to his father at Iddesleigh and soon managed to collect a small pack of foxhounds, 'hunting', as he said himself, 'anything I could find around my own garden'.

Six years later he was appointed Perpetual Curate of Swymbridge and Landkey and he moved his household and kennels to Tordown. His income increased to £180 but out of this he had to pay a curate for Landkey, meet personal expenses, pay for his son's education and meet numerous calls on his generosity from a large population of poor parishioners. During the forty-five years he was to remain there, he had the parish church restored at the cost of £3,000, new schools built and a new chapel erected.

The parson was noted for his kind heart and love of animals and was in return loved by all who came in contact with him. He was a special friend to the Romany tribes and they repaid his many acts of kindness by helping him in turn. He is said by Charles Castle, who wrote a most informative article about him that appeared in *The Field* on 28 January 1950, to have been a deeply devout man, morally strict and, unlike many of his fellow churchmen of those times, he had very little use for wine and an abhorrence of tobacco.

During his time at Tordown, he became famous for the strain of terriers he was producing and, seeing the price that his friend Mr Wootton was prepared to pay for wire-haired Fox Terriers, there is no doubt that he could have added considerably to his income if he had sold some of his dogs. We have no records of him selling any, only of those he gave away. His dogs were devoted house pets as well, so he was loath to part with any of them.

After Penelope Russell died in 1874, Lord Poltimore offered Russell the living at Black Torrington and for financial reasons Russell was forced to accept. A recent book about the Parson states quite mistakenly that he did not breed any terriers after he moved there. I have been able to photocopy, with the kind permission of Count de Pelet, letters written by the Rev. Russell from Black Torrington dated December 1881 and 1882 in which he talks about his dogs and his breeding problems when some of his bitches failed to have puppies after being mated and 'other of the young ladies' failed to be mated although he had used Willie, his best dog, on a Rags daughter.

John Russell refused to sell his terriers to Methyr Guest to help himself out of financial difficulties. In response to Methyr Guest's suggestion that he sell him some of his terriers and let him have the necessary breeding stock to cover £400, throwing in his hunting horn as well, John Russell wrote 'I will not sell them to you. I never do sell them but I will give them to you.' This supports the point that his closest friends and grand-daughter Mrs Mary Russell maintained: that John Russell always gave his terriers away, and so confounds all those writers who call him a dog dealer.

We are told that the terriers that were bred out of the same litters as those that were made into show dogs, started to evolve into two very distinctive types: smooth- and rough-coated, and some had shorter legs than others. None of the dogs we see pictured with the Parson was short in the leg, but he gave some away to a Miss Ellis who bred from five of them, continuing to do so for many generations, and some of hers were much shorter-legged than her original stock.

It must be borne in mind that Parson Jack did his breeding and hunting nearly fifty years before the Kennel Club was established. He was a Founder Member of the Club and a leading Fox Terrier judge; what was considered a good terrier in those days would not merit a second glance today and the same can be said for most of the other breeds that can be found in the pages of 'Stonehenge' and similar dog literature of those times.

However far the present-day working terrier may differ from those bred by the Parson, it must be remembered that few people require them to enter against foxes. If they did, a ten-inch 10lb. terrier would be no possible adversary for a vixen, let alone a big dog fox, and it would be the greatest cruelty to expect one so tiny to venture against a badger. (Badgers are now protected by a new Act of Parliament.)

In the next chapter we are going to try to ascertain what qualities and characteristics make up the present-day version of the Jack Russell Terrier; how it compares with those the Parson originated for his own very special purposes and if he really would be turning in his grave at the unkindly described 'monstrosities that have been perpetuated in his name'. We shall see if he would forgive them their looks in consideration of their gameness, toughness and indomitable spirit and if he wouldn't have a little bit of fellow feeling for them because of their great delight in his own favourite sport. Perhaps he would forgive them their short legs when they show him their ability to draw an earth and their readiness to enter it regardless of what they may encounter. He would be the first to appreciate the fact that terriers who get taken to a meet in a van don't need the length of leg that his own had to have to be able to keep up with the hounds.

2 What is a Jack Russell Terrier?

Here's Devon and Somerset's Terrier Pack!
Every one bred from 'Lynton Jack'.
Narrow and straight, with natural coats,
Possessing pluck worth many groats.

English Life
Arthur Heinemann (1925)

The question 'What *is* a Jack Russell Terrier?' is a much harder one to answer than would at first appear. If questioned, most people would have met one, seen a picture of one or grown up near one. When asked to describe this well-known 'breed', everybody's description is contradictory to everybody else's. They disagree about colour, size, coat, markings, character and vices, but all are describing the same 'breed'. All know they are describing a Jack Russell and no other breed.

John Russell's Own Standard as narrated by the Rev. E. W. L. Davies in his biography called *Memoir of the Rev. John Russell:*

> TRUMP
> In the first place the *colour* is *white* with just a patch of dark tan over each eye and ear, while a similar dot, not larger than a penny piece marks the root of the tail.
> *The coat*, which is thick, close and a trifle wiry is well calculated to protect the body from wet and cold, but has no affinity with the long rough jacket of a Scotch terrier.
> *The legs* are straight as arrows, the feet perfect;
> *The loins* and conformation of the whole frame indicative of hardihood and endurance;
> while the *size* and *height* of the animal may be compared to that of a full-grown vixen.

Russell bought Trump from a milkman in Marston near Oxford and Rawdon Lee says that every possible endeavour was made by him and others to trace this milkman or the possible breeder without success. Evidence of an excellent strain of terriers in that area shows Trump may have been bred by an expert. In any case she turned out to be the foundation of all his famous terriers, in fact the grandmother of Tip one of his most famous terriers in a long line that lasted until Russell's death in 1883.

Mr Joe Copping, Founder member of the Shires Jack Russell Club, Breeder and Judge, with Tiger, his 14″ Best in Show winner.

After John Russell died people started saying that he was nothing more than a 'Terrier Dealer' and would take and breed from any sort just as long as it was a 'game' one and looked a likely looking dog. There is, however, no record that Parson Jack ever sold his terriers. There is plenty of evidence of those he gave away – namely 'Pussy' to Tom Wootton who in turn sold him for £40 to Mr Shirley, founder of the Kennel Club. When we say 'likely looking' we can be sure that it was the size, shape and conformation that John Russell admired. He was obviously clever at picking them out. Capt. Percival Williams of Scorrier wrote in 1956 that John Russell used to stay with his grandfather, George Williams of Scorrier House in Cornwall and on leaving would enquire if he had any terriers to spare. He would be told that if there were any in the kennel that weren't wanted he could have them. He would then collect terriers from anybody who had any to spare. I only quarrel with the word 'anybody'. It is quite certain that Squire Williams had a very good strain of terriers and that John Russell had probably had a hand in their breeding himself, as the two men were such friends. Capt. Williams admits that the strain of terrier had been in his family for over a hundred years. The Rev. John Russell was no fool, obviously. He needed terriers too even though he had given up his hounds in the 1870s. When he stayed with friends in Scotland or elsewhere he would send up a couple of terriers by way of thanks. They would be asked to choose the one they preferred and send the other on to another friend who had been Russell's host. 'Fill the crate with potatoes' when you send it back was all the payment Russell expected or asked.

Fanciers like Murchison, Redmond, Turner and Gibson paid large sums for their terriers and charged accordingly. When Burbidge, the famous cricketer and terrier breeder died his kennel of 'Hunton Strain Terriers' realised the huge sum of £1,750 for his executors. John Russell was equally famous and his terriers were in the Hunton strain background through Old Juddy and so on. There is no such sum published after the Rev. John Russell died. He, poor man was forced to leave his beloved Swymbridge next to the Exmoor he loved to ride over, and start again at the very end of his life. Swymbridge, by the way is the very next parish to Chittlehampton where my husband's parents were both christened and married. Three times a week John Russell passed across their land Whitestone Barton when he hunted in that direction. Some of the family walked hounds for him – one was known to have put a dirty mark in the middle of a clean tablecloth and the maid covered it over with a vase of flowers. I can find no record of his terriers in my visits although I stayed in the George Inn in South Molton, where John Russell and his friends had their famous Club.

John Russell died a poor man, and even in his will his terriers were to be *given* to all the people who were named in it.

Alys Serrell had obtained some of her hunt terriers from the Parson and later on she was joined by Augusta Guest MFH of the Blackmore who was left some of John Russell's terriers.

Countess Howe's grandfather was a great personal friend of John Russell. He was Mr C. H. Basset of Watermouth Castle near Ilfracombe. Countess Howe said that Mr Russell left a good many of his terriers to Mr Basset when he died. They were carefully bred and Countess Howe could remember seeing them. 'All of the same shape and size not high on the leg or long in the muzzle, but they were game.' Her grandfather kept very careful records of his terriers and bred them for a great many years. She knew that Mr Russell did too because she had seen one of his pedigree books. Joan Begbie another breeder of Jack Russells from Dorset wrote that her grandfather Henry Searle had his terriers (not bought) from Parson John Russell and she grew up with them. She thinks the blood is greatly diluted but thanks to the late Arthur Heinemann, who bought up every drop of blood in the form of every one of John Russell's terriers he could find it was at least preserved. Alice Harris, née Rawle – granddaughter of old Wilf Rawle John Russell's kennelman, worked for Heinemann at his Porlock Kennel. He was a MFH and she took over this duty when he went to war in World War I and was the first secretary of the first Jack Russell Club. Mrs Begbie is sure that the Parson kept very careful records and this was confirmed by Miss Serrell and Miss Guest. Miss Serrell in her book *With Hound and Terrier in the Field* described how she used John Russell's breeding and the results she got.

A Miss D. Ellis was left five terriers in the Parson's will but some of hers are short on the leg.

Miss Mary Russell one of John Russell's five grandchildren said that she often used to stay with her grandfather and knew all his dogs. He didn't have a smooth-coated one when she was there. She knew he kept careful records for she had seen his many pedigree books and such. After his death papers were found blowing all over the grounds of his home. Some pieces of his famous sermons were picked up and it was thought his dog records went the same way. His solicitors did not have any and would not have put much store by them if they had them. It was very unfortunate that his only surviving child should die soon after him so that more care wasn't taken at his death. After Heinemann died in 1930 Alice Harris went to work for the famous animal author H. Williamson and she produced a large packet of papers, diaries and such and said that she would give them to him if he would write them into a book about the Rev. John Russell. He decided that it wasn't his type of book and declined and nobody knows what happened to all those papers.

People who know next to nothing about quite popular breeds of pedigree dogs often have a considerable 'knowledge' about the Jack Russell. When told that there is no such breed, they refuse to believe it and quote names and places up and down the country – not just in the country, but in towns as well – where they have come across the breed. When told that there is no such breed *registered* with the Kennel Club, they look at me pityingly and quote chapter and verse. Obviously they think I am out of my mind not to know the breed and, if the Kennel Club do not recognise the breed, it must be the Kennel Club who are at fault.

Having been told time and again that the Kennel Club do not recognise the breed, I approached the Kennel Club to find out why these particular dogs have been for so long on the wrong side of the fence.

The Kennel Club is to the canine world what the Jockey Club is to horse racing – its governing body. It has the final word in all matters of dog showing and is the keeper of the register of every pedigree dog that has ever been registered in this country. Without the Kennel Club, there could be no pedigree dogs because it is a fact that the Kennel Club vouches for the three generations of breeding behind dogs which makes them 'pedigrees' and not just names on pieces of paper.

As a breeder of pedigree dogs, later as an exhibitor and finally as a judge, I have always gone to the Kennel Club if I ever needed advice and have always found them ready and willing to help, so I took up this matter of the non-recognition of the Jack Russell with them and the reply I was given was informative and could be of considerable help to

(left:) The Duke of Beaufort with one of his terriers. His family established their Badminton strain in the early days for work purposes.

(right:) David Lloyd George with his favourite terrier Grock and a corgi named Dai.

anybody who feels that the dogs have not been fairly treated.

Mr G. Baker of the Kennel Club was very generous with his time, giving me the Kennel Club's point of view and the reason why all previous applications to get the breed accepted had met with refusal.

I have twice been a Founder Member of a new breed club and found the Kennel Club very helpful in getting these established once the initial refusal to recognise a new breed that did not altogether meet with their approval was overcome. So knowing the way the Kennel Club works, I enquired just what would have to be done in the case of the Jack Russell in order to meet with a more sympathetic response.

I am going to set these answers down here as if anyone is anxious enough to heed Mr Baker's words and follow his very wise and sensible direction with a view to resolving the difficulties and straightening out a lot of misunderstandings, there is no doubt in my mind that within a certain time it will be possible to establish a breed acceptable to the Kennel Club and still recognisable as the trim little terrier we often see nowadays – said to be a Jack Russell Terrier.

We should be glad that there is such a body as the Kennel Club to hold the reins. If they did not demand such a high standard and were not so very particular about the dogs they have registered, British Dogdom would not hold the high place in the world it does today.

Mr Baker told me that between the wars there had been a Jack Russell Club which even had a 'standard'. In 1948 Mrs Jim Harris (née Rawle) was Secretary and a noted breeder and exporter of the Jack Russell.

The standard compiled in *Dogs in Britain* by Clifford Hubbard, who is one of the leading authorities on dogs in the present day and is perhaps best known as the editor of the *Observer's Book of Dogs* – one of the most widely read dog books – says that the Parson Jack Russell is a game and varminty earth dog with which few terrier bench champions dare compete.

> The head is broad and powerfully muscled at the cheeks; the eyes are dark and medium in size; the ears are set high and carried dropped over to the front or side; the muzzle is powerful with even mouth.
>
> The body is medium to long, firm and straight in back; the chest is rather narrow and not very deep; the legs are short and straight, well-boned and with hard-padded round feet; the tail is set high and docked fairly short.
>
> The coat is short, thick and close, usually wiry in texture although some smooth-coated dogs appear occasionally in litters. Colour is white, predominating with tan, black or lemon points on the ears, above the eyes and on the set-on. Too much black or tan is disliked, as white is the most useful colour when the dog is working with hounds against fox or otter. Height is 14 inches and weight is 16lb. for dogs and 14lb. for bitches.

Clifford Hubbard goes on to say that, unfortunately for the reputation of the breed, some breeders of Fox-cum-Sealyham Terriers, which have no intrinsic value, sell their stock as Russell Terriers, which has caused more than one writer to confuse the genuine article with the spurious, with the result that he declares the Russell dog to be a mongrel of no importance.

Probably the fact that the idea of the Jack Russell was just what so many people wanted for themselves explains why many of them were not fussy about showing their dog or even breeding from it. Unfortunately, there were not many pure-bred Jack Russell Terriers to be found just after the war ended in 1945, so people took what they could find. Wherever they came from, any poor type of Fox Terrier, especially if low to ground, was passed off as a genuine Jack Russell Terrier. Some, I regret to say, owed something of an admixture of

Dachshund or Corgi blood and so numerous did they become that they completely over-shadowed those game, sensibly bred little terriers that were manfully striving to keep the good name of the Parson Jack and his true type of terrier with the matchless blood of his famous Trump.

Vernon Bartlett writing in *The Field* said that he had seen a toy smooth Fox Terrier with prick ears that had been sold and accepted in good faith as a Jack Russell. Even if the pup's parents were 'the best to ground for miles around', he said, 'that still does not make him a Jack Russell but a hunt or working terrier.'

Vernon Bartlett started his article by saying:

> Recently my fellow, but famous, Devonian, the Reverend John Russell returned on a short visit from Elysium where he tells me he has enjoyed good hunting since 28 April 1883.
>
> He appealed to me to request the hospitality of your column in which to protest strongly at the many queer animals sold today as Parson Jack Russell Terriers by 'cashers-in' on his name.
>
> He asked me to send you his own specification of 1871. I am also to say that a good picture of a real Jack Russell appears in the *Observer's Book of Dogs*.
>
> Devon's most famous sporting parson was born at Dartmouth on 21 December 1795 [*author's note*: I am writing this paragraph on 21 December 1974, just twenty-one years short of two hundred after the Parson's birth, and his name is still remembered and his memory respected] and save for his Oxford days was never outside his beloved Devon for longer than ten days at a time. He built his wonderful terriers from local material – i.e. the old, game Devon Terrier, improving wherever he could with outside blood, *Trump* a particularly fine Devon Terrier, being one outstanding example.
>
> There is no shred of evidence to the contrary [but see page 00] and, as they say in east Devon, 'it stands to sense.' Today there are dozens of good working terriers, but few of them are Jack Russells which must, repeat must, be around 14in. and 16lb., with straight legs and a thick, rough coat.

Mr Bartlett ends by saying that the right sort can still be bought if one seeks hard enough in its own native land. Meanwhile, one should avoid any puppy which does not fit the specification.

When I asked Mr Baker what had become of this old strain he told me that there had been some attempt to revive it but the efforts seem to have died out and nowadays the dogs he saw answering to the name of 'Jack Russell' were extremely diversified in type, especially with regard to size, shape, colour, coat and ear carriage. *They varied so much that they could never be grouped together and called a pure breed*. Mr Baker told me that this was explained to the Jack Russell Terrier owners when they applied to have the breed accepted by the Kennel Club as a pure-bred race.

This was understandingly disappointing for the owners of the real Jack Russells, but there can be little sympathy for the owners of first-crosses, who must surely realise that it takes a good many generations of breeding like to like before a breed can be said to have even started.

There is no reason, of course, why there should not be a breed of small working terriers built on the lines laid down by John Russell and, if two good and typical specimens could be found of each sex and they were bred together and the resulting litter was level for size and type, very close in colour, markings and texture of coat, then the sexes could be bred together out of this same litter an a definite strain would start to emerge. Providing all the people who are breeding Jack Russells accept the standard set down by the Parson and all breed as closely to it as possible, this will hasten up matters.

The Jack Russell Club
A Club was formed in 1975 for the avowed purpose as stated on the form:

> The Jack Russell Club of Great Britian has been formed by people who want to keep the breed pure, continuing to possess the courage and instincts it has at present and to maintain a register of Jack Russell Terriers.
>
> Membership Fee £2.00

The first secretary and founder was Mrs Romayne M. Moore of Exeter and the Club held its First Indoor Show on Sunday 26th October 1975 at the 'Dog Centre' Stoneleigh which was on the ground of the National Agricultural Centre, Stoneleigh, Kenilworth, Warwickshire – which when it was first chosen was said to be in the very centre of the country.

There were 14 classes – puppies of mixed coat, smooth puppies and rough puppies, restricted classes for Club members with mixed coats, Best Dog with Working Certificate given by an MFH which had to be produced, and the same for Bitches; Best Brace, Best Veteran and the Best in a class that had not won a prize on the day and the Best in Show was judged by the two judges, Mr Tom Normington of the Grafton Hunt and Mr Vernon Bartlett, the well known West Country judge.

For a fee of 30p per class prizes and rosettes were on offer to four places. It is usual to have two judges in the ring at a time one a Hunt Servant and the other a knowledgeable amateur.

Mr Ray Cutler's smooth Russell Bitch Trim, winner of the *Shooting Times* and *Country Magazine* Perpetual Shield at the Great Yorkshire Show July 1987.

Australia: There is a Jack Russell Terrier Club in Australia and they are a very lively Club and have picnic meetings every month or so. They have a panel of judges and often have shows in conjunction with Hound and Hunter Shows. They also have terrier racing.

One idea that springs from the fact that they find importing stud dogs so costly as they have to pay for quarantine like we do, is that they have syndicated stud dogs and semen banks for artificial insemination purposes.

When this book was first published I was asked by a breeder in Australia to send her a supply of semen from the Jack Russell in Liz Cartledge's arms. Unfortunately this was a bitch and has left the country anyway.

U.S.A.: There is a Jack Russell Club of America and they give registration certificates and register their dogs.

South Africa: A lot of Jack Russells live in all parts of South Africa as they are particularly adapted for the hot climate being more rugged than some breeds. I am told that every time they go out into the garden they pick up ticks and they only like smooth coats.

There is a lot of ignorance shown in the way owners of Jack Russells are afraid they will lose their zest for work if they become show dogs. This didn't happen in the case of spaniels who all had to win their championship in field trials before they could become show champions. The same thing could be expected of any working terrier that he must show his working certificate in order to be a show champion. Terriers are born to hunt and as long as they are given the opportunity to do so they won't ever forget. It is the owner's fault if once his dog starts going to beauty shows he forgets to put him to his rightful work. Modern veterinary knowledge is such that any cuts and scarring that might occur as the result of encounters with his usual adversaries can be healed up so quickly that they can hardly be thought of as a deterrent to a show career.

What is important is that all the owners of Jack Russell Terriers have the interests of the breed at heart and start thinking about breeding for soundness as well as purity in order to perpetuate a race of little terriers they can be proud of and not a race of cripples. This does not mean that they have to forget the importance of the working qualities but that they make correct construction equally so.

Overseas breeders are in need of a proper working blueprint to breed their Jack Russells by. They look to the parent Club to produce this and it is vital that agreement is reached and a serious attempt made to produce a Standard that can be put forward to inform the very serious breeders who have taken up the breed that has been exported to them. Without any official backing there is nothing to make such a standard the one and only one and new clubs with different breed standards can spring up all the time. It is a very big advantage that once a breed is accepted by the Kennel Club and a standard submitted to it that immediately becomes the official standard for that breed all over the world. Every other Kennel Club abides by it and judges have to judge by it, so breeders are forced to breed to it. From time to time breeders find that their particular standard omits something important, is not clear enough or needs improving in any way. There is nothing to stop this happening and any alteration to the standard, once agreed by a Club that the Standard needs adjustment there are proper regulations under which this can be done and the Kennel Club notifies these amendments to all the other Kennel Clubs.

From its inception the Jack Russell Club of Great Britian was very well supported, many hundreds joining almost at once. They have a scheme for registering litters by drawing in markings on a chart but even so it doesn't make them pure bred as the aims of the club state they wi .. Anyone can send up the markings of any type of cross-bred if they wished to do so and there is no compulsion for Jack Russell owners to join the Club as they can show their stock at Breed Shows and any of the Working Terrier Shows. The office work required is as heavy as the Cattle Breed Clubs who have highly paid experts to compile their Stud Books, which have now outpriced themselves in almost every case. This could soon eat up into the club's finances and could take so long to produce that it may be out of date when it does arrive.

At any rate the Club grew so big it was necessary to decentralise it and now the Jack Russell Club of Great Britain is split up into areas.

The Jack Russell Reform Club was set up to try and bring the breed within the confines of the Kennel Club and this is prepared to work for this end. I was invited to be a Founder Member of this movement and was pleased to do so. Although only too well aware of the value of this little dog as a worker to want to stop it working in any way, I feel the owners of Jack Russells are in an invidious position and it is one way to do something definite. The hundreds of people who bought a Jack Russell don't want to be able to charge more money for their pups, they want the little dog that they are so delighted to own to have its proper place in the scheme of things.

It is not clear as they stand at present if they are even allowed to call themselves 'Jack Russell' in view of the stringencies of the Description of Goods Act. It will need a test case in order to sort that problem out.

Before the Kennel Club accepts the registration of a club, it requires to know that there are twenty-five founder members who had paid £2 each towards founding the club. This payment is only required when the breed is accepted as a pedigree one. Anyone can form a club and if it is to promote a breed of dog, there is no need to make a large subscription – just enough to cover expenses. Meetings and rallies can be held, however, and only good can come of a number of people meeting to discuss the breed. A united club will have a much stronger voice when the time comes to put their case to the Kennel Club and a much better chance of getting it accepted.

They are, after all, dealing with a terrier in a terrier group and, whatever alien blood might be found behind it, it will only be another terrier. The worst that can happen is that the dogs will come too short, or too tall, have poor markings or too many markings, and – one of the most argued points – whether the coat is to be smooth or rough.

Many adherents of the original Jack Russell quote that there never was a smooth coat in any of the Parson's packs of terriers (in fact – see page 39 – there were a few.) This was a wise choice in view of the bleak, cold nature of the terrain he hunted. Smooth coats are more vulnerable to chill winds. Also the extra coat gave them protection against damage from teeth and claws.

That rough coats will appear in smooth bred litters and probably vice-versa is certain. When one coat is found to be recessive to the other, the time will come to breed complete litters all of one coat. Until that fact is proved, the coat will have to be registered according to how it looks, as has been done with Chihuahuas and Griffons and other breeds where one coat is recessive to the other.

The achievement of uniformity is not far beyond the reach of the imagination. It is certainly more likely than could have been thought when we consider that Bulldog and the Great Dane – such opposing breeds – should be used together in the development of the magnificent breed known today as the Boxer.

I had my first experience of owning a terrier similar to the breed we are considering in 1945. It was given to me by a neighbouring farmer in Berkshire. Her dam came from the South Berks Hunt and as my little bitch had a spot on one side of her body we called her Decimal Point. She was the keenest thing after rats and rabbits we had ever known and whatever her breed, she would have won admirers for her courage. She was shorter on the leg than the Jack Russell we have been discussing, otherwise she conformed surprisingly. I did not know her breed, but when people stopped to admire her, they always referred to her as a Jack Russell and we were quite happy to call her one. Although given to me, she soon found that she got more satisfaction in my husband's company and accompanied him whenever he went out on the farm. She had great spirit and would follow the gun all day.

Many of our friends and relations admired her so much that they asked for puppies from her so I tried to find a mate for her and this caused quite a problem. The only male anything like her in size and shape was a rough-coated dog belonging to a local farmer. For some reason, the dog refused to mate her.

Then somebody told me that the Duchess of Newcastle had a barn full of terriers just like mine, so I got in touch with Her Grace and was duly invited to tea. I took my little bitch along and the Duchess was not at all impressed. 'She's not very pretty, is she?' she said. I said that I thought she was very pretty and I was particularly anxious to mate her to the dog Her Grace showed me, as it had such long legs. We had quite a friendly argument and, in the end, the Duchess took me out to an enormous barn that had been converted to house her collection of about sixty Fox Terriers. Jack Smith, who, managed the kennel for her, brought out a few dogs. In the end, we mated her to Call-over of Notts.

I would like to be able to report that from that mating, Decie founded a dynasty. I regret to say that this was not the case. The eventual litter was a great disappointment. All had peculiar heads, huge umbilical hernias and the little mother did not like them a bit and deserted them almost immediately. I had my first experience of hand-rearing and they took calf's milk substitute readily enough; I tried to get them goat's milk and was only able to obtain it occasionally. I eventually gave them Guernsey milk from our own herd, but either it was too rich for them to digest or I may have been too generous; they blew up like balloons and before they were three weeks old, they died.

The stud fee had been three guineas but I decided I would not use another pure-bred Fox Terrier again. The Duchess of Newcastle and I remained the best of friends and I often visited her at her home in Ascot, sometimes driving over in my pony and trap, as petrol was in short supply at the time. Her constant companion was a tiny, faded black rough Griffon with the quaintest expression. It was such a delightful little dog with such a sense of humour that, instead of increasing my interest in terriers, I soon decided that I must have a Griffon.

When my little terrier needed a mate next time, I found a dog that was so like the pictures of the Jack Russell Terriers bred by the Parson himself that he might have been related. I met this dog being walked over our fields. I liked the cut of him and he was quite willing to mate my bitch. The resulting litter was a fine one of seven and they were a lovely even lot – lightly marked on nearly all-white. One was very like the mother and I gave him to my father-in-law on whose farm he lived for thirteen years.

I kept a dog who was longer on the leg with a clean cut head, beautiful shoulders, very light markings of black and tan on the head and a white body with a black circle round the tail. His ears were neat and he carried them folded forward; he had the most intelligent expression and when I had him docked, he looked such a handsome little pup that we christened him Toff. He was one of the most stylish dogs we ever owned and over the years I have bred quite a few

Judging hunt and working terriers at a county show.

champions. As he was an unacceptable type, it never occurred to me to get him into any breed. He stood against the champions and looked just as smart. We never thought of him as a mongrel, and when he went out to woo the local talent – which he did quite often – we were always proud to see his offspring in the village. So many of them had that peculiarly distinctive circle round the tail. He had a charming character, never fought with my other males and how he loved to hunt! He would go missing for days and often came home with a thick piece of root across the roof of his mouth which meant he would have been caught underground and had to chew his way out. To the end of his fourteen years, he had beautiful teeth.

Whatever mixture of blood produced him, I wish it were possible to find it again as when he died we were never able to find another to take his place and I don't expect we ever shall. Although he looked smart enough to be a pure-bred show dog, he was an earth dog before all else and lived only to hunt and work. More than anything else he loved to go out with the gun and he would point and always show where the game was, like any trained gun dog. If nobody was hunting, he was quite happy to go off by himself and he had a special bark when he had found something. Another trait that connected him with Jack Russells was that he would run on three legs when he was tired and change the leg which was resting. This is a characteristic that has long been connected with the strain.

One line that Toff was responsible for is still going strong. I used to dock Lady Smith of Cowslade Farm's Jack Russell Terriers and on one occasion I noticed a very pretty tan and white smooth coated dog with a broad head, neat ears, sound front and a delightful temperament. I told a neighbour about her as she wanted a dog to run with her ponies when her children went riding. Polly filled just this need and became a much-loved family pet. Mated to Toff, Polly produced four puppies, three dogs and a bitch, christened Spot, who was retained to keep her mother company. When it came to mate her, we used a Jack Russell Terrier called Dudley. I intended to buy the bitch from this litter but the owners moved before the pups were weaned and I lost touch with them.

Polly came back for another mating to Toff and I was pleased to take a puppy instead of a stud fee. I got Posy who was very smart and pretty as paint with a black and tan head with a wide blaze.

3 The Character of the Jack Russell Terrier

Considering the breed is not officially in existence, it is remarkable that all the people who say they have Jack Russells all have the same sort of stories to tell and the same characteristics to describe. So, even if the strain is quite diverse in its looks, at least the terriers are all as like as peas in pods as far as their ways and habits are concerned.

First of all they are sporting, active little dogs with a love of the fields and open spaces. A walk round the block to the pub at night and a slow dawdle round the shops or with the baby's pram is far removed from the life they like to lead. They have the capacity for keeping up with hounds over some pretty rough hunting ground. They will crawl through bracken and very thick undergrowth and their skin seems to be thick enough to withstand some of the tears and scratches that so beset the whippets when they go through hedges. They can cover many miles in a good day's work and so they need fairly extensive exercise every day and not just once a week. They can be sublimely happy on a golf course but this joy is not shared by the people in charge of the greens! They love to dig and the hole already made seems to be an open invitation to add a few more! It is better not to take them to a golf course, as if they are made to remain in the car while their owner is playing and walking round the course, they will suffer such frustration that they are likely to make off on their own if a door of the car is opened inadvertently. They can of course be taken round the course on a lead.

As a house pet, a Jack Russell makes a loving, happy little companion who will enjoy all the family activities and join in any fun that may be afoot. He is devoted to his owners, is brave in defence and mostly non-aggressive.

His intelligence is such that he hates to be confined to the house or shut away anywhere. He can endure the car because it means being with the people he loves, but he will like to watch out of the window and get very excited when he sees another dog. Travelling with these terriers is never dull but can be a bit of an ordeal!

The dog I had for fourteen years was a friendly, loving little fellow who would go wild with delight when we set off on a tour of the fields around the farm. With his tail in the air and his nose to the ground, he

A smooth-coated Jack
Russell with a lovely
face and intelligent
expression.

would investigate every burrow and thicket on the way and show his pleasure by running back to us periodically. Walks with him were full of interest and for every mile we walked he would cover three or four.

I never saw him frightened, although a contretemps with our aged gander during the terrier's younger days gave him a healthy respect for that formidable foe and he always gave him a wide berth. It came about that one severe winter the geese were fed mash in a trough in the farmyard. Because it was so cold, the mash was mixed with warm water and it gave off a savoury smell. This intrigued Toff, who was pottering about the yard, and he went over to the trough to get a taste. He had only just put in his nose when George the gander appeared and in fury grabbed the intruder by his tail. Geese have serrated beaks which give them a very good hold on anything they are gripping, as Toff found to his cost. They both weighed 12lb. and so neither gave an inch. They might have been there for ages for we were all busy on other parts of the farm. Luckily my husband heard Toff's cries and, thinking he was having trouble with a rat, went to his rescue. He had a hard job prising open the gander's beak. Ever after that Toff avoided the geese and wouldn't go near the trough again.

Sir Arthur Bryant wrote a charming description in *Jimmy; The Dog in My Life* which was published in 1960. He tells how Jimmy adopted him and his wife on a Cornish cliff in 1942 during one of Sir Arthur's leaves from war work. He described Jimmy as a rough-haired English Terrier who, if he did not conform to the pedantic requirements of any breeding society, had everything proper about him if viewed purely as a dog. He had a snow-like coat which, when brushed and washed, was almost dazzling white; large and well-proportioned brown and black spots, a short 'stuggy' brown-tipped tail that usually, like his aspiring spirit, pointed perkily upwards; long graceful legs that, with his stout heart, could carry him swiftly; two satiny brown ears that sometimes lay in repose and at other times pointed upwards like the pavilions of a medical army; and, concluded Sir Arthur, the most beautiful brown eyes he had ever seen.

He tells how Jimmy had come to watch them eat their sandwiches and obtained two for himself so expertly that he showed himself to be a professional at begging. He was not owned by any of the local people and had spent the summer begging from picnic parties on the cliff and catching rabbits. He attached himself to Sir Arthur and his wife and followed them back to where they were staying. On the way, he showed himself to be very friendly with all the other dogs he met; in fact, he could be said to be the soul of amiability and there was not a hint of fight in his manner – he was said to be the spirit of universal charity.

After some deliberation, Bryant and his wife approached the police and offered Jimmy a home, and so he made the journey to their house in Buckinghamshire by train and taxi which he took in his stride, and then made his mistress's bed his own sleeping place for the next fourteen years. The most surprising thing was that as soon as he found that he belonged to a place of his own, he changed astonishingly quickly from an almost barkless, gentle creature into one who was also embarrassingly vocal, with the lordliest airs and a pugnacity towards every creature bigger than himself that would have done credit to a Red Indian on the warpath. He became at once a boss dog and let the world know it. Never was terrier more a terrier, more challenging, more enquiring, more restless than this one that so dominated the Bryants' lives. He didn't wait for challengers but looked around and joyfully invited them.

Yet – and this was the pathos of him – a harsh word, a stick raised to chastise, a suitcase packed for a journey he might not share, and all the confidence went out of him like water drained from a cup. His tail went down, his head hung and a look of unutterable sadness came into his big brown eyes. Even chocolate, which he loved above all other foods – most inconveniently, seeing it was rationed – would remain untouched at his feet if his mistress went out without him. To her, for all his fierce challenge to a world which had tragically misused him, he gave a love as single-hearted and unquestioning as any Bryant had ever witnessed.

He was a dog that always wanted to be off somewhere and, despite his great love for his owners, he could not resist the longing for adventure. A window had only to be open or a garden gate ajar for him to be through it and off. He would attach himself to any passing stranger or follow a scent across a field travelling at his quite remarkable speed – he could out-distance a bicycle – and soon be far away beyond recall. There would then follow hours of agonised searching and much telephoning to neighbours and police, and often long after nightfall he would be retrieved by his long suffering mistress. He always returned with every manifestation of passionate devotion and contrition for having left, and he always greeted his rescuers with frantic delight and would return home barking with excitement. His other favourite pastimes were hunting and fighting.

I have described Jimmy and recounted some of his history because it is so close to the description of my own Toff and of many other terriers known as Jack Russells. He might well have been related because he certainly had the looks that the Parson described so vividly and his character and failings so closely resembled other owners' tales of their terriers. Cornwall is the next county to Devon and the drawings of Jimmy by David Rook show him to be much nearer a Jack Russell than a wire Fox Terrier.

Some owners complain that their Jack Russells are vicious and bad-tempered. I was told that those obtained from the hunts were a snappy lot and did not make good pets. This surprised me for I have known many delightful terriers that came from hunt kennels and they have been very sweet-tempered. On enquiring further, I was told that many hunt servants get landed with all sorts of terriers that people cannot cope with because of their bad temperament. If they are good at the work, they are often, unfortunately, bred to the detriment of the stock. Actually, a breeder of some very famous working strains of terriers told me that he would not allow any fighting or bad temperaments in his pack as it interfered with the work and set them off against one another instead of at the fox.

Some of the more bad-tempered ones seem to prefer going after squirrels or rats. This spoils them for fox hunting. They must never look at rabbits and such when fox hunting. These hunting terriers have hunting so imbued in their blood that they often go off on their own or stay in the earth so long or go so far inside that they get lost. The Fell and Moorland Working Terrier Club was formed with the aim of supplying help for rescuing terriers that get trapped in this way.

The various hunts up and down the country nearly all have their terrier pack, and hunt servants breed and have a ready sale for their stock. None of the people I talked to in this particular field was interested in getting the strain registered at the Kennel Club. Their reason was that the tendency would then be to breed for looks – in fact, to in-breed – and they felt sure that they would lose the intelligence and indomitable character of the breed. They were quite content with the classes and judging that went on at the Hunt Terrier shows.

Another side to the character of these little terriers that has now become an accepted part of those Hunt Terrier shows is 'terrier racing'.

A terrier is at its happiest when rummaging amongst the undergrowth.

This started in Ireland about twenty years ago and is proving very popular with owners and dogs who join in with extreme enthusiasm. Mr Tom Bruder of Guildford has a portable track, and the dogs are let out of traps and chase after a rabbit skin. They go over fences just as veritable little steeplechasers and great fun is had by all, especially the excited onlookers.

'They're off!' The Shires Jack Russell Terrier Club really enjoy their racing.

A little hunt terrier was hunting one day when he vanished and, despite all efforts to find him for a fortnight, he was considered 'missing – probably dead'. While hunting the same area two weeks later he was suddenly seen to be hunting with the hounds and was apparently fit and well.

The T. V. News announced that Cindy, a small Jack Russell had fallen down a mine shaft. Miners had been trying for days to reach her and so had the police, the local fire-brigade and an R.S.P.C.A. Inspector had been let down on a rope but they had all failed to reach her. Her cries were pitiful and were getting weaker and weaker so after much thought it was decided the only thing to do to prevent her suffering more and dying slowly of starvation was to blow her up with dynamite. This they did and her cries were heard no more. Sadly they returned to their homes. Imagine their surprise when she returned to her home – thinner and dirtier, but at least alive. The explosion had blown up the part where she had been imprisoned. She was able to dig through what was left and although she emerged in a totally different area from the one she had been in before, she found her way home in no time. These little terriers have an uncanny bump of direction.

A terrier in full flight.

All football supporters will remember the relief felt when a little Jack Russell unearthed the valuable and so highly regarded World Cup some time after it had been irretrievably lost.

Somerville and Ross summed up the terrier in *Experiences of an Irish R.M.* when they wrote: 'It is indeed almost with awe that one reflects on the greatness of soul and the self-respect, the self-consciousness (a quality that is attributed erroneously, I believe, to man only) of a very small terrier. Especially are these present in the terrier that is accredited to a pack of foxhounds. When it is considered what it can accomplish with that tiny body, those indomitable little legs, that absurdly small head, packed with constructive intelligence, yet with a brain-pan no bigger than an apple, it is impossible to deny that its opinion of itself is justified.'

Whatever name we like to give this astonishing little terrier, it cannot be denied he would still be just as popular with the discerning buying public who have taken him to their hearts despite the fact that he goes unregistered by the powers that be and unrecorded in almost every case. To do this, he must possess qualities far above the average for a household pet and companion, even if he were primarily invented for work in the hunting field. It must be admitted that he has won his place by his own efforts and many charms. All owners of these merry little dogs will recognise their own in the apt descriptions quoted above which are only just a few, but I could have filled this book and over with stories of the exploits of hundreds of others as recounted by their enthusiastic and proud owners.

4 Buying and Caring for the New Puppy

When it has been decided that a Jack Russell Terrier is to be acquired as an extra member of the family, it is essential that a good deal of time and attention is given to finding the one most likely to meet with your requirements and the one most capable of fitting in with you and your family. This is most important for it is hoped that he will be part of your family for twelve or fourteen years — which is the probable life expectancy of Jack Russells who are brought up and looked after with love and common-sense. Before these long years are lavished on the wrong dog, it is sensible to look around and find the one most likely to bring you satisfaction and companionship and one that seems gay and intelligent so that a mutually happy state of affairs can be achieved.

The Bad Choice

It may be amusing to return home one day with a pathetic little bundle whose pleading eyes and shivering mien you had been unable to resist when visiting the pet shop for goldfish food, peanuts for the birds or some equally minor item. Your friends might think you a kind and sympathetic sort and you will hope the dog so appreciates your kindness that he will be your willing and obedient hero worshipper for the rest of his life. These sentiments may not be shared by the other members of your family, who may not join you in your pity for the forlorn creature. Their pity is for the one who has to clean up his messes and other even less pleasant evidence of the unhealthy state of his stomach.

By the end of the first month, you might have had to spend quite a large sum at the vet's, but by this time you are probably 'hooked' by your terrier's quaint little ways and his constant look of rejection every time he is put out to learn his house manners. By this time, too, you will have spent so much money on inoculations that, even if he makes everyone's life a real misery, you just can't afford to give him to the dogs' home or to those nice old-age pensioners you know in the village who will give him a very good home but lack the means to buy him.

So you buy him a collar and have his name and your address engraved on it. That is the end, so far as you are concerned. He is now your dog and because of this you might have to put up with years of the dog's ill-health, his staying out at night, biting the postman and

All puppies are adorable.

barking hysterically when everyone in the neighbourhood passes the gate.

Had you had the good sense to see where and how he was bred, it should have been possible to discover his bad temper, revolting manners, bad morals and ill-health by close examination of his background. The pet shop owner is in no position to know and could not have helped you. Common-sense would have shown that the dog's parents were not likely to produce anything good or intelligent and the way he was fed and brought-up generally would have revealed many short-comings.

He might have seen his parents biting people they disliked and so he will probably do likewise. He might bark a great deal if his mother was unhappy and barked a lot when she was looking after her litter. She would probably have been mated every season and so her pups would suffer if her constitution was undermined by constant breeding. It is unlikely that she would have been fed the extra vitamin supplements and extra food that it takes to keep a feeding mother in good enough condition for her to feed the pups and still keep up her own strength. Without this extra nourishment, her whelps would suffer and probably be taken away from her as soon as they could fend for themselves.

There won't be much pleasure, either, in owning a dog who runs and hides under the furniture every time you have a visitor, or one who shows his teeth and snarls when you try to pull him out. Biting the hands that feed him shows that something is very wrong indeed. Biting the postman and milkman could be considered 'legal tender' and he may be allowed to get away with it once, but he may not be given a second chance.

Many poor, misguided fools are going to have a sense of failure because they cannot make the dog the affectionate pet they so much want. They will struggle on perhaps for years, telling themselves that only they can possibly understand the poor creature. Their proper course would have been to have returned the unfortunate pup to the shop from which they obtained it and ask for a credit note. The shop keeper knows that few people taking a puppy home to love will admit failure, so he bases his business policy accordingly and takes unfair advantage. Of course, not all pet shops do this but there is a certain section that does, otherwise there would not be so many dogs that soon find themselves thrown on the mercy of charitable institutions because they have been bought by people who have not known better.

It has been known that if a newly bought puppy is found to have fleas, lice or other unpleasant but quite curable conditions, the owners just abandon it without any guilty feelings. Any vet of the R.S.P.C.A. or P.D.S.A. will give the necessary cure and the charge will be minimal. A puppy from a well-regulated kennel should not have any skin afflictions because the necessary precautions against them will already have been taken. The same thing applies to worms. These should have been dealt with by the breeder before the puppy is ever available for sale.

As I have said above, not every pet shop is as bad as the one I have made an example. Some have very high standards, will not accept puppies without knowing their backgrounds and will be ready to give you plenty of advice. You can usually tell what a pet shop is like by just looking at the animals and the cleanliness of the floor, etc.

The Correct Choice
A healthy puppy from a good breeder and a clean kennel should be sold free of all the faults mentioned above. In fact, for an extra few pounds you can have a vet's opinion and a certificate stating that, at the time of sale, the puppy was in good health and was not the harbourer of any skin or internal parasites. At ten to twelve weeks, the puppy should be vaccinated as protection against hardpad and distemper, hepatitis and leptospiral jaundice – to name but a few. If it is found necessary to take the pup younger than this, it can be fully protected for six months at least with a correct dose of measles vaccine. Personally, I am against puppies going to new homes before they are eight weeks old and buyers are unwise to insist that a six or seven-week-old puppy is necessary to fulfil a birthday or anniversary present. Far better to give the collar or even a book about the breed on the special day as a forerunner of what is to come, than drag an unweaned baby from its mother before it is old enough to look after itself.

The sensible buyer decides which breed will best suit his family needs, the size of his house and car and, not least, the size of his pocket. The time available for grooming and exercising must also be considered. If the family is garden-proud, it should be remembered that a Jack Russell needs to dig, so either the choice of breed should be changed or the Jack Russell will have to be accommodated where he won't upset the happy harmony of the gardeners, but still be able to dig away to his hearts content in a bank or rough piece of garden where his efforts will cause no annoyance. It won't be easy to keep him off the flower beds as these have special attraction for him, but early training and firm adherence to this training will be needed. If he is allowed access to the garden on some occasions but not on others, he will not understand. If he is *never* allowed in the garden proper under pain of severe scolding and perhaps a rolled newspaper flourished in his face when he attempts entry, there is more chance of his understanding the position.

As this breed is not one that comes under the jurisdiction of the Kennel Club, which is the best authority to consult when buying a puppy, and which will supply lists of names of creditable breeders, it will be necessary to consult the more sporting of our periodicals for advertisements relating to this little terrier. *The Field* and *Horse and Hound* are two which usually have litters advertised and sometimes the local hunt will know of likely puppies available or being made available in the near future. Leaving your name and telephone number and stating your interest may take time but is quite likely to bring the desired effect and, in course of time, news of a Jack Russell litter will come your way. There are few neighbourhoods nowadays that do not have at least one or two breeders who specialise in these terriers but I am trying to give the best advice to someone who does not know the breed or have any experience with buying a dog.

Any two breeders may contradict each other as to what is the *proper* Jack Russell Terrier, so it is better to look over a wide area. The more you see, the more you will learn and the extra experience will help you make a wise choice. This is important because the pup *must* fit in with your particular background and way of life. If you have a house full of rowdy, jolly children who are wanting a similar companion so that they can all romp and be happy together, don't buy the quiet one of the litter. If you live in an upstairs flat and do not wish to annoy your neighbours with a dog barking, get one whose parents rarely bark, and get a bitch as she won't need to go outside to relieve herself so often and will be able to hold out longer than a male.

When choosing a bitch that it is intended to breed from you must be careful to select one that is well up on the leg because if she has short legs she will carry her unborn litter with the greatest difficulty and has great trouble when going up and down steps as the underneath part

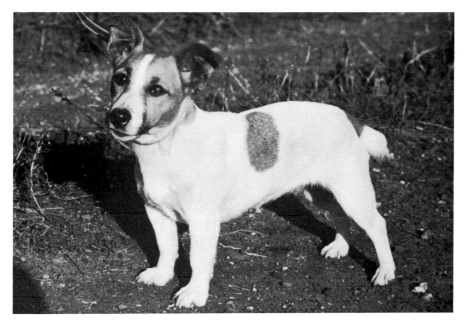

Midge, an example of a very good type to choose for working.

keeps banging against everything she walks over and is particularly awkward when there is a large litter because the weight will drag it down to the ground bumping them along when she moves. You wish you could find a sling of sorts to take up the weight and keep the whelps out of the way.

It is best to be very particlar about such matters so that when it comes the time to breed from her you will have to choose a sire that has long legs, is bred from longer legged parents and who is known to produce puppies the majority of which are 'on the leg'. Make sure his parents are well up on their legs and try to see the grandparents to check for this. There is such a preponderance of short legged dogs in this breed that it could be due to the short legs being inherited as a recessive factor. It would mean that two short legged terriers mated together will only breed short legged ones too. And this would continue for as long as this policy was adopted. If long legs do appear sometimes this could mean that long legs are recessive to short ones. Long legs then mated together will always breed long legs, but if when two short legged ones are bred together the litter contains one or more with long legs then it is possible that the short legged ones are carrying long legs behind them as a recessive gene, and they will appear in litter after litter in the same manner. Now by mating two long legged terriers together who are both carrying this hidden gene for long legs, all the resultant puppies will be long legged. It is essential that such breeding policies are practised under the guidance of a genetic expert, such as they have at the Kennel Club or similar bodies whose advice they have at their command. The newly acquired computer will also do an incredible amount of the brain fag and record keeping so that it will in fairly quick time possess a breeding pattern showing exactly what genes Jack Russell breeders are playing with.

I speak from experience for many years ago when I had the staff and the money for such costly experiments I set about trying to establish if there was a recessive gene at work in the Chihuahua. After generations of all smooth breeding, while trying to fix the wonderful head of a stud dog I had imported from America, when mating him to his own daughter, I produced the first long coat I had ever seen. There was nothing to mate her to so I kept her as a pet. She broke her leg so couldn't be mated anyway and by the time she was recovered her mother's litter sister had bred a long coat dog. I mated these two long coats together and produced one of the best long coat Chihuahuas of all time – not my description. I had nothing to mate him to as I felt I was dealing with a 'mutation' so experimented with the bitches I had at home. Mated to any of the bitches he was related to he produced smooths and longs but not any pattern – 3-1 at one time and 4-2 from the same bitch later. I was sure that he was only siring long coats to his relations because they both had the same common factor for this type of coat. It was necessary to import another stud dog to have unrelated bloodlines and I managed to buy a long coat bitch from a quarantine kennels whose mother had been mated in Mexico so I had some complete outcross blood. Every time my first long coat was mated to the long coat import she only had long coat puppies. Every time my long coat stud dog mated the Mexican bitch they only had long coat puppies. I mixed them all up, keeping to the long coats only and generations later I was still getting long coats. Long coat bitches mated to my dog from other breeders were found to breed true as well. I waited to find out how other breeders' experiments were getting on but nobody else bothered as they found that by mating longs to smooths they were getting 'show stock' and that is all they were looking for. Everybody kept mixing up the coats and nearly 20 years later they are still doing so and now that the Kennel Club wishes to split the two coats into two separate breeds they are frightened to stop their cross-breeding. However I was able to prove my point that long coats were recessive to smooth.

Using the same dominant/recessive factor I tried to find if size in poodles could be treated in this way – was miniature size dominant over toy size? No picture of any sort appeared but I discovered that apricot mated to apricot from as many different strains that could be found would always breed true.

Taking the point as far as the Jack Russell is concerned what is

Liz Cartledge with
her very typical
hard-coated bitch.

wanted is for someone with a broad view of the breed as a whole – not just its working capabilities. But, seeing what poor shape some of them are in if they couldn't be boasted about from their gameness there is precious little that can be said in their favour. And this type will go on appearing when they are bred for nothing more specific. It will need a dedicated group of people who have all got the same commitment. The Jack Russell, after a period of coming together when its Club was formed is now being split up again into separate little corners where nobody will know what the other lot are doing. It will never become a breed of any standing this way; it must be a National Body elected by as wide a membership as possible and with power to vote the way the majority wish.

If this so-called Jack Russell breed decides to go it alone and not belong to the Kennel Club, then there is a tremendous amount of responsibility to be shouldered to promote this breed the way its large number of paid up members have a right to expect. It will need rules and have enough authority in its governing body to enforce them. A rigid standard with every detail of the Jack Russell described in detail so that breeders all over the world can breed to it and judges everywhere understand it and judge strictly to its outlines.

The governing body must liaise with all its fellow clubs in all parts of the world and representatives must visit regularly to maintain good fellowship and make sure that they are breeding to the standard as laid down by the Jack Russell Terrier Club.

Every such club must be listed and informed of every change in the standard, rules and policy.

Judges will need to be trained to such a high standard that they can go to all the overseas clubs and judge their terriers satisfactorily while visiting judges from abroad will have their fares and hospitality all paid for by the Club.

A three generation registration system with transfer and export forms and a stud book with the names of all the Club winners and all the members names is required and all working certificates recorded.

The bills for all the shows will have to be met so running such a large undertaking will be very costly.

Having made the all-important choice and having found one that seems to want to belong to you, the biggest obstacle is over and it only remains to get the puppy home and start a daily routine that will be to everybody's advantage without putting all the strain and responsibility on the shoulders of one person in the house. Everybody's dog must be everybody's responsibility. If his care is shared equally, everybody will benefit and the dog will share his affection all round instead of keeping it exclusively for the one who looks after him most and being a nuisance about the house to other members of the family.

Early Feeding

The puppy should arrive with a diet sheet explaining how he has been fed up to the time you bought him. Although this does not have to be followed exactly, it will be a good guide and will list all the things that are essential for his well-being. It is better, in the early days, not to change his diet too drastically. Although he may have been fed raw meat and you wish to feed him tinned or prepared food, you should continue his usual food for a time and change over very gradually as and when he takes to the new tastes and methods of cooking.

My personal theories are based on raw meat and natural feeding with added vitamins and mineral supplements so that the dog gets a daily supply of every item that his body needs to resist disease and to grow and develop to the best advantage. At the end of this section, I have given this diet so that readers can use it if they wish. You should bear in mind the facts that dogs being brought up for the purpose of breeding and which must be able to pass on good constitutions to another generation, are going to need a more fortified diet than a household pet.

Meat, milk, biscuits or brown bread make a good diet for all house dogs, and as extras they can be given brewers' yeast and charcoal which keep them healthy and with sweet breath. They will pick up extra goodness from certain plants outside and if household scraps are saved and incorporated in their daily food intake, they will never have any deficiencies. If scraps are handed out *ad lib* whenever the table is being cleared, or food which the children don't want to finish, a dog will not need a regular feed. Whilst the scraps might be adequate, it is far better to establish a routine feeding time and never feed at any other time.

With the present cost of food, there are not as many meaty scraps as there used to be. But if there is a lot of wasted meat, fish or eggs, place them in a dish and when feeding time comes, supplement it according to it contents. You may only need to add a handful of biscuit meal and a little gravy, or some extra meat may be necessary. If there is a lot of bread, potatoes or other carbohydrates in the dish, add meat but cut out the biscuits.

A normal healthy puppy will make good progress fed this way. He needs milk and cereal for breakfast, meat for lunch, milky tea with toasted bread rusks for tea and cooked meat with puppy meal for supper. Four feeds up to twelve weeks, three feeds up to four months, two feeds up to six or seven months and one feed daily thereafter. Thin dogs may need two small feeds a day to keep them in good condition, and fat dogs should get one small feed daily. These fat dogs will benefit greatly from a weekly fast day when they should have a rhubarb pill on the evening before, a whole day without any food and then an early feed of normal size and quality the next morning. But you should never do this while the dog is still growing as they need a good daily diet to grow and maintain their development. It is of more benefit to a dog living an over-fed, under-exercised existence – the lot of so many pet dogs today.

Terriers are active little dogs and Jack Russell Terriers have long association with ancestors who have been bred to have 'staying power' while out for a day's sport, either digging into the earth or chasing the fox above ground and keeping pace with the foxhounds, who are reputed to be the fastest of our British hounds – apart from the greyhounds who are not used in chasing the fox.

It is wise to feed your puppy at regular four-hourly intervals to begin with, then five-and-a-half-hourly, and, when on two feeds a day, at eight in the morning and six at night. When on one feed a day it should be given at the best time to suit the family arrangements generally. It is better to make the dog fit into the family times than the family having to change a long-standing routine for the sake of a dog. Using common-sense all round when looking after a puppy can be more of a joy than a chore.

It is just a matter of dividing meal times according to the puppy's growth. When he is older, he will not have to grow so much and then will need less food – only, in fact, a maintenance ration which should consist of some milk, some meat and some carbohydrate. After the second teeth have come through at about five months, the milk can be diluted to half-milk and half-water or one of the cheap milk powders can be given if economy is necessary. Biscuits can be replaced by brown bread baked in the oven and fed dry. Large marrow bones should be allowed as these are very helpful in providing the jaws with the exercise necessary to allow the natural juices of the saliva to dissolve some of the bone calcium which adds greatly to the nutritional value of the bone. Teeth will be kept clean and healthy by this means and there will be no need to clean them with a brush and powder.

DIET FOR A JACK RUSSELL:
A healthy Jack Russell will require about 10–12oz. of food daily. Some of it should be in the form of 'hard tack' – bones, hard biscuits, baked bread etc.

A growing puppy will need twice as much daily but when the stomach is small it must be divided into three or four meals spaced through the day.

The daily diet needs to contain 80–150 calories per kilogram of body-weight each day. When working, more energy is used and the calories need to be increased accordingly.

1lb. Meat: 800 - 1,600 calories according to its quality e.g. muscle meat is best and tripe and offal lower.
½lb. Biscuits: 1,000 calories.
Fats (Butter, Margarine Milk etc.): Vegetable Oil or fat meat at least 5% daily. This will provide energy but needs reducing in an older dog but increasing to 15% for a growing puppy.
Calcium and phosphorous: Found in bone meal
Sodium Chloride with potassium is essential: Found in most organic foods unless thrown out after cooking. Use all vegetable water.

Vitamins A, B, C, D, E, and K are required daily and all trace elements, minerals, etc. found in SA37.

Raw oatmeal has one hundred times more calorific value than cooked porridge.

The most nourishing foods are beef, mutton, chicken (only half as good as beef) herrings, liver, cod, eggs, tinned foods for protein. Cheese is high but needs mixing with bread or any other cereal to balance.

Cereals can be – in order of food value – bread, biscuits plain or mixed which are often more valuable with the addition of proteins, raw oatmeal, cooked oatmeal, rice.

For fats, butter is way above everything else, next comes lard, cheese, milk and fish oils and vegetable oils all of which substances supply the necessary fatty acids the dog's system requires. Bread and butter and milk is a terrific meal.

Water always, bones for teeth and some special treats like cheese, boiled liver or vitamin sweets to aid training by way of bait are all very necessary.

FEEDING CHART FOR PUPPIES

8-12 weeks — 4 feeds a day

8 a.m. Breakfast	Farex or Readibrek or other baby's cereal with warm milk and glucose.
12 noon Lunch	Raw minced meat with SA 37 (see page 74), a little suet and a little chopped *cooked* liver. A small meaty bone to chew. Cold water to drink.
4 p.m. Tea	Lactol biscuits fed dry and a drink of milky tea or Lactol.
8 p.m. Supper	Cooked meat or fish, scrambled egg or other protein food with about one-third added puppy meal moistened with nourishing gravy.

13-16 weeks — 3 feeds a day

8 a.m. Breakfast	Cereal such as Weetabix or Readybrek and warm milk with glucose.
1.30 p.m. Lunch	Raw meat cut up small, with small quantity of *cooked* liver or heart and SA 37 added. Meaty bone to chew. Cold water to drink.
7 p.m. Supper	Household scraps or cooked meat or fish with one-third added puppy meal moistened with gravy. Saucer of half-milk half-water until teething is finished.

4-7 months — 2 feeds a day

8 a.m. Breakfast	Milky cereal with glucose.
6 p.m. Supper	Raw or cooked meat, including household scraps, with biscuit added and gravy. Drink of milk/water if liked. Large bone to chew.

Water should always be available in the day.

Full details about feeding your dog after the age of seven months will be found in the section of General Feeding on page 77. If your puppy still seems to be rangy at seven months, continue with two feeds a day but *do not* let him get too fat.

Inoculations

It is more than likely that your puppy will arrive from the breeder with a certificate of inoculation. But if he has not recieved these, you should take him to your vet when he is about ten or twelve weeks old which is the time he loses the immunity he has gained from his mother's milk. He should be inoculated against distemper, hardpad, hepatitis and leptospiral jaundice. Nowadays these are all combined in one injection, with a second dose of lepto usually given two weeks later. There is a new killer disease called parvo virus rampant in this country and abroad that can only be controlled by cat enteritis vaccine.

You should not let your new puppy wander outside the confines of your own garden until he has had these injections. Do not let him out on to the pavement as he could easily pick up one of these dreaded diseases. It is advised to have booster injections every so often as a precaution and I certainly think it is worth the cost of them rather than bear the horror of the illnesses. In fact, most reputable boarding kennels insist on seeing a vet's certificate giving the date of the last inoculation and may refuse to take your dog if they consider it has not received a booster recently. They have too much to lose if disease breaks out in their kennels.

Indentification

Every dog must have a collar with his name and address on a metal plate or on a disc which can be attached to it. If you have a telephone, it is a good idea to add the number as well. For dogs out working, where a collar could cause them to get caught up, you can have your telephone number tattooed inside his ear or in the groin. Special firms do this for you. The disadvantage is, of course, if you move house! There is a firm who for a small fee will tattoo a number on him which they record for identification purposes and this will be his number how ever many times he moves house.

5 General Care and Feeding

Once the dog is about seven months old, he will be more or less fully grown except that he will fill out a bit. His training will be well under way and hopefully he will be turning out to be just the sort of dog you imagined when you bought him as a two-month-old puppy.

General Feeding
A dog fed on house scraps and added meat, fish and eggs with bones, bread, vegetables and fruit will not need to have his meals changed to make a variety as there will be such a wide choice in any household diet. If he is fed on tinned food – and the majority of dogs are nowadays – you should try him with several brands in case there comes a day when the particular food you use is not available. If he is not used to different brands, it may take a dog quite a long time to adjust to something new. Present-day dog food preparations are very sophisticated and, according to the labels, contain all your pet's needs. This may not be true in times of stress, such as breeding or growing, and special attention should be given to a dog's requirements at different times of his life. For instance, in winter, he needs more carbohydrates to keep his body temperature level. Extra biscuits should be given, but *never* sugar as this does harm to a dog's teeth and serves no useful purpose, unless there is a sugar deficiency or some sort of comatic condition when sugar water is a very effective remedy.

If a dog gets injured in the stomach or has a serious illness which makes eating either painful or impracticable, a vet might prescribe a substance called hydrolised protein which, if given with the help of an eye-dropper, will keep the dog alive for weeks without having to eat solids. I used it in a case of meningitis for six weeks, and at the end the dog's poor old brain had got better and he lived a happy and productive life for another nine years.

Old dogs do not need extra food to keep them happy. Quite the contrary, in fact, since as they get older they become less active and so need less food rather than more. A surplus of food will make a surplus of flesh. The diet that can be supplied by the vet to reduce his obesity will cost you twice as much as the original food would have done. By far the best policy is to halve the food when you halve the exercise. This way, your Jack Russell will live much longer and have a much happier and more active life. The weight of surplus fat alone is enough to make an old dog extra tired which will then form a vicious circle so that in the end he will probably die from an over-tired heart that has failed to pump hard enough to send the blood flowing through his body. This will be a mechanical failure but it will be just as deadly as if he were run over by a bus.

Very old dogs lose their teeth but this need not inconvenience them much. They can attack minced meat with gusto and, as their stomach juices are so strong and can dissolve the meat even if swallowed without chewing at all, no harm seems to have been done. Bemax or All-Bran added to the meat will help keep the intestines happy by supplying roughage and this will help avoid anal gland trouble, a menace where meat-only dogs are concerned. His eyesight will benefit from Vitamin A which is found in halibut oil and, if cod liver oil is mixed with it, his skin and coat will not get the dry scurf so often associated with age in the dog. Salad oil because of its unsaturated fatty acid quality is one of the best cures for scurf on the skin. One or two teaspoonfuls daily will be all that is needed. Even quite serious diseases like diabetes and glandular conditions can be treated efficiently these days. Close attention to the vet's suggested diet and a course of the pills applicable to the disease are proving that dogs as well as humans are gaining longevity as a result of the increase in medical knowledge.

The diet I suggest for a household companion will not be an ideal one for the working dog because of the nature of his work and the long hours he will have to spend outside in all kinds of weather, and he must have extra carbohydrates to give him extra energy.

In most hunt kennels, a lot of oatmeal porridge is used. This is cooked with sheep heads, offal and tripe. The more affluent kennels have a mincing machine and everything the slaughter house has to offer is mixed in. In hunting country, it used to be the thing for any farmers belonging to the hunt to offer any casualty animal and still-born calves

(left:) Mary and her litter mates. Even at such an early age the difference in coat texture can be noted. Suitable feeding dish and hairbrush are shown.

(right:) Feeding time; five to a dish is too many and feeding from separate dishes is much better.

and these were a very welcome addition. Nowadays there is, I am afraid to say, not quite the *rapport* between the farmers and the hunts that used to exist. Meat is expensive, but with the help of an increase in followers most hunts manage to feed their packs adequately and the little hunt terriers come in for their fair share.

More information about general feeding will be found in the previous chapter and in the chapters concerned with breeding.

Water

Plenty of clean fresh water is essential as it is food as well as drink to a dog. Dogs who are fed on the 'dry' ration as a number of them are these days must drink water too or they will die.

When your Jack Russell leaves an earth he is always very thirsty and will appreciate a drink when he comes out.

Bones

Where there are plenty of rabbits, these are very good to feed to your terrier but *never* feed him any bones as they easily splinter and cause the most terrible internal damage. Poultry bones are just as dangerous. Burning them or disposing of them in rubbish bins is better than burying them in the garden as your wily little Jack Russell will soon dig them up. Naturally he will bury his marrow bones all over the place but it doesn't seem to matter how long a bone has been buried or how very revolting it seems; chewing it appears to do him no harm.

It might be a good time to give a warning about him digging up bones on a farm or any other property. Sometimes foxes are poisoned instead of being killed by the hunt. The carcasses are buried and if the poison used was strychnine, it will remain in the bones for as long as they are about. Your Jack Russell is likely to die a swift and horrible death if allowed to dig up and then chew what he has found.

Compost heaps should be wired off as these are favourite play-grounds of terriers and they attract rats and other vermin. Once your dog finds rats in the compost, he will give the heap no peace and the rotting-down of matter for the improvement of your garden will be a thing of the past. However domesticated he may become, the blood of the Jack Russell will out and he will soon revert back to the busy little worker he once was.

As a character, he is easily bored and if no means are available for him to give vent to his feelings, he may chew furniture and carpets, destroy shoes and gloves and put the house into chaos. Keep some dried *marrow* bones around the house and these should always keep him happy. These bones can be bought from the butcher and once he has taken off most of the meat in the garden, boil off the rest of the meat (or if possible, cook it in a pressure-cooker) and when the bone is dried it will not smell or be in any way messy.

If you do not give him a good bone to chew, he may turn into the local wanderer and soon get himself a bad reputation with the local police as a danger on the roads, a sheep and poultry worrier or maybe even a 'killer'. Keeping him under control will take a lot of ingenuity. My neighbour moved house with three dogs, one of them a wandering type of Jack Russell. Before the new fences were erected, she tried everything to keep him at home, but without success. One day he had been more adventurous than usual and, as it was a glorious day, she did not feel she could shut him indoors. While she was busy elsewhere, she tied him to the garden spade which was so deeply buried in the earth that she couldn't move it. A bit later, we heard a most peculiar clanking noise coming from our drive. Presently, the dog appeared over the hill and arrived in our courtyard panting for breath, having dragged the heavy spade weighted down with a mass of soil all the way!

Car Travel
If a large *dry marrow* bone is provided for the dog to chew during a long car journey, he won't be nearly as ready to be car sick as if he is looking out of the window at the objects flashing by, which is one cause of travel sickness. Fright or just nervousness at the change of routine can also act on a dog's stomach – especially a puppy – and give him a tendency to drool, and this is the first stage of a condition that will spoil many a car journey. A comfortably lined box on the floor with the bone will occupy him fully for the first part of the journey, allowing his body to become accustomed to the prolonged motion and vibrations he must endure for a long time.

If a bone proves ineffective, a travel pill can be given half an hour before the journey begins. Milk and glucose should be given as a feed and nothing else. It is better to feed a dog at the end of a journey.

Never allow a dog to travel with its head out of a window. This is very bad for him and may cause a chill in the eyes or a foreign body to become embedded in it.

When stopping at a place where the dog is not allowed out, make sure that two windows at least are left open so that a through draught keeps the air in the car moving. If this is not done, the car will become like a hot-house. You should *never* leave the car parked in the sun. Even if there is only very little sun about, what little there is can quite quickly distress a little dog and maybe even cause him to die of heat-stroke. To save a lot of trouble, special window guards can be obtained which lock into the opened windows so that the car cannot be broken into and the dog cannot get out.

If the dog becomes a good traveller but suffers from tummy rumbles because he is hungry, a hard-boiled egg is an excellent meal for him on the journey. It can be carried in its shell and is clean and easy to feed; it just needs mashing up roughly and can be fed quite quickly off a paper napkin.

Grooming

It is a good idea to let the children of the family attend to the dog's daily grooming. Children of even six or seven years are able to wield a hairbrush and comb. If this is done daily, it will keep the hairs in the comb instead of on the carpets. Twice a year, the Jack Russell Terrier will lose his coat and there will be hair all over the place – dark clothing and car seats being the most annoying places to find it. Most dogs moult in this way at the change of the seasons and there is not much that can be done to avoid it. Feeding kemp or seaweed meal as a daily diet supplement will stop the coat moulting in ordinary circumstances as there are many Jack Russells that lose their coat continuously. This is often corrected by the addition of vitamins to their diet and Vit. B complex is also of use.

The rougher-coated variety is the most difficult of all and the sooner the dead and dying hair is got rid of the better. The best thing is to start by bathing him in a sulphur solution. Sulphurated potash has the most loathsome smell but, if you put two ounces in two gallons of fairly hot water, it will dissolve and then it should be cooled down to blood-heat and the dog soaked in it for ten to fifteen minutes. If he has any suspicion of skin disease, the solution can be left in the coat and will be found very effective against mange, mites and similar irritations. It will dye his white parts bright yellow so if his skin is healthy it should be rinsed off with luke-warm water. When you comb – a very fine flea comb is ideal for this particular grooming – it will be found that a quantity of hair will come away. This bath removes the dead and dying coat and what he has left will be found to be young and strong and not easily pulled out.

The moulting season is the best time to strip out the long straggly hairs that make some Jack Russells look 'something or nothing'. If these hairs are removed with the finger and thumb of the right hand – the other way round for left-handed people, of course – the hairs, if pulled one or two at a time, will come out quite easily. The head must be stripped short all over, but the eyebrows can be left on as well as a beard and moustache. Ears should always be kept neat with no growth of hair visible. It is better for a woman to perform this part as men find it too tedious and in any case they may pull too hard!

From behind the head and ears, down the neck as sleekly as possible, remove the coat until it lies close to the body. Strip the body down tight to the elbows. Keep the hair on the body short but finish off with

A very even group of
rough coated terriers.

slightly longer hairs on the legs and round off the feet. Kept this way, it will only require a couple of hours attention every few months and if he is fed with seaweed and fish oils, his coat should hardly shed at all.

A really heavy-coated Jack Russell will probably need professional stripping twice a year, otherwise he will look like a shaggy hearth rug. If no professional is available don't whatever you do, let your local vet's staff run the animal clippers all over him, which is what often happens in'busy surgeries, where they have got the staff and the know-how but not the time to spend hand-stripping a terrier. There is, after all, no real reason why you shouldn't do the job yourself providing you have the will to succeed. It is a long, laborious task if you want to do the whole job at one sitting. As an inexperienced performer, your fingers will get stiff, your back will ache and your poor little victim will also get very fed up. It is better to do the job gradually.

Start with the tail – all terriers are used to being pulled by the tail and pulling out the loose hairs will not hurt your pet at all. It is best to bath the dog before starting as this will get rid of the grease on the hairs and make them easier to grip. Rub your fingers on a chalk block or in powdered resin, which is the professionals' favourite, comb the hair on the tail away from the skin and, if you are sitting in a good light, you will see that some hairs are longer and coarser than others. All these

Unusual speckled markings on a smooth coated Jack Russell bitch (which needs more neck).

have to come off, one by one, not two by two to start with. Take thumb and first finger and just pluck them out as if you were plucking a chicken. Pull the way the hair grows and if you hold the dog on a sheet of plastic paper, it will save the hair messing up your floor and is easier to usc than newspaper. Cover your clothes with the most impenetrable clothing you have as dogs' hair gets in all the crevices.

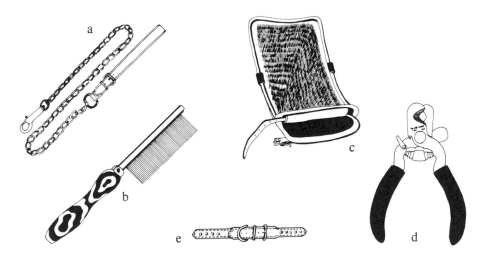

Fig. 3 Grooming kit: (a) chain lead with leather handle and swivel locking device; (b) fine-toothed comb suitable for grooming terriers; (c) hound glove; (d) the latest in nail cutters with a special safety device; (e) collar

Puppies need playthings or they will help themselves to something – in this case a brush.

When you have finished the tail, you can stop for that session if you feel you've had enough. Never 'square off' the tip of his tail with scissors! You will find that the hair over his rump now looks most odd and, having just got into your stride, you may decide to go on with the job. Combing the hair upwards, take the longest ones first and work across the back from left to right and back to the left again. Do try to only pull one hair at a time as once you start pulling out lumps you will lose the shape very quickly. When you have had enough, stop at the end on the right hand side. Next time you want to start again, you will see exactly where to begin. Work from the top of the left leg to the top of the right leg. When you reach the stomach, work from the tuck-up on one side to the same spot on the other side. An hour or so of this will seem pretty tedious and you may need to have several sessions but, because you are working to a proper pattern, he will look quite presentable in between. You will be able to see by this time how much nicer his undercoat looks – all sleek and lying flat with a correct look about it. He will be well covered but so neat that you will be delighted with yourself and may want to finish the job despite your sore finger and thumb.

When you reach the forelegs, you must find the point of the elbow and strip every dead hair above it using a line to the bend in the foreleg as a guide line. All the hair across the chest needs to be stripped down to the undercoat but if there are some crowns on the front, as there are crowns on the rear, these will be difficult and the hair may be left longer. Neaten off with thinning scissors, but never ordinary cutting ones as they will show ugly 'cut marks' which spoil the effect just as much as clipper marks, and uneven work spoils the appearance if they have been used instead of the hand-stripping method.

Continue stripping up the neck, keeping in even rows as much as possible until you reach the back of the skull. It is easier to take all the dead hair off the face and head when you first start but, as you grow more experienced, you will want to experiment with leaving eyebrows and a beard. It is hard to learn from the written word. You will need to see it done or at least the finished article. Ears should be stripped of all long hair, to be like velvet.

A stiff bristle brush and a fine-toothed comb are all that is necessary to keep a rough-coated terrier in a well groomed state. Five minutes or less a day, once the stripping work is done, will keep all the loose hairs at bay.

A hound glove or a little bristled pad that can be buckled round the hand is an efficient tool to use on smooth coats. A daily brush-over will keep the coat gleaming and make it uninhabitable for fleas etc. Unless a smooth coat is plastered with dirt or moulting badly, bathing is unnecessary. If the dog is allowed to romp in long grass, especially when the dew is on it, and has a daily smooth-over, the coat will always be gleaming.

If a bath is necessary, it should be a cream one with an insecticidal agent. Detergents are too strong and harmful to a dog's skin but Stergene is good if there is any dandruff. The special baby shampoo that does not smart the eyes is a good one to use on the head. If you are bathing the dog for the first time, the pup is sure to fight and it is very difficult not to get suds in the eyes. The head should be done first and rinsed with clean water and dried before starting on the rest. Be very careful not to let any water in the ears which could be harmful. If the pup is placed with his back feet in the sink and his front on the draining board, he will not be so frightened. Use tepid water only. If it feels warm to your elbow, it will be too hot for the dog. Rinse in cool water and towel off quickly. If he can shake himself really well several times, a lot of the water will fly out of his coat. To make him shake to order, blow gently down his ears.

When the weather is very cold or if a bitch is expecting puppies, or if you want your Jack Russell to look especially clean, it is a good idea to dry-clean him with cornflour. There are dry-cleaning blocks, liquid sprays and alcohlic foam on the market, but none as safe, cheap or effective as cornflour. Take him outside or into a shed and, using a flour sifter, powder the dog's coat thoroughly and rub it in well. Leave it on for half an hour or so and then brush it out vigorously. It will be found to leave the coat with an excellent shine, very clean looking and, surprisingly enough, it will not shake out all over the place like talcum powder and chalk.

As Jack Russells are such diggers, it might be necessary to bathe earth and other foreign matters out of the eyes. Cold tea, boracic lotion or proprietory eye-drops are all helpful. For really inflamed eyes, an eye ointment is necessary. The vet will prescribe one and it is good to have a reliable one always handy.

If the ears get chapped – the edges get hard and red or they get thickened – they should be massaged well with Vaseline. Vaseline is also the best remedy for a hard, dry or cracked nose. It should be rubbed well in.

No dog can look well groomed with long toe nails which, besides making him look shoddy, also hurt enough to affect the way he walks. After bathing is the best time to cut them as they are soft and not so likely to split. Proper nail cutters must be used. Scissors are impossible and only split the nails. Great care *must* be taken not to cut below the quick. This is sometimes quite near the surface and if the nails are black only, the sight of the blood will tell you that you have gone too far down. The dog will also tell you but it will be too late then. Peroxide of hydrogen or iodine will help stop the bleeding and prevent infection, but it is a very unnerving feeling for the dog and must be avoided. Regular road walking or a rough file – a piece of carborundum is helpful when rubbed one way only – keeps the nails short.

While on the subject of feet, they should be regularly examined in case grass seed gets embedded between the toes and any thick mat of hair in the pads is best removed with curved scissors. Tar on the feet is very unpleasant indeed. Rubbing butter well in or a good soaking with turpentine will help. But tar is best avoided and you should not let your dog walk on tarred roads when the sun is hot enough to melt it. Eucalyptus oil will remove tar if it gets on the skin or the coat.

Remove mud from pads between toes by soaking the feet in warm soapy water. Stand the dog in a bowl or the kitchen sink to do this as it will take time for the mud to soften. Treat icicles or hard snow which may stick to a longer coated Jack Russell, in the same way.

Exercise
It must be realised that the Jack Russell is a terrier, a working terrier at that and one quite capable of keeping up with the hunt pack during a full day's hunting. Although many of the little short-legged terriers that grace the name of Jack Russells would find this difficult, they are still quite able to cover five miles of very rough ground on a country walk and then be ready for a strenuous game of ball when they return. Down to the shops and back and down to the local and back is simply not enough and it would be hard to keep one content with this limited exercise. If that is all the family are willing to offer, they would do better to buy a toy breed or a small poodle that will exercise itself quite

happily by inventing games and racing round in quite a small space. Jack Russells like to walk and run and run and run.

There are quite a lot of Jack Russells that are used for racing and very fast they go over a short distance – and over hurdles too. This form of sport is often seen nowadays at terrier shows.

They make ideal companions for long country walks – inquisitive and busy the whole time, their enthusiasm for the hedgerows and the ditches soon becomes infectious and a walk without a dog after the interest of their company is miserable. Their company is never dull or boring. They find something new every turn of the way; they disappear from sight down dubious-looking holes and reappear quite unexpectedly somewhere else – their tails wagging nineteen to the dozen and their breath coming in sharp little barks of excitement as they try to tell you what they have found underground.

You can be walking along quite calmly and all of a sudden the dog might stop, put his head on one side and listen; then stick his nose in the ground and start to dig furiously. Every hole is different and is greeted with renewed excitement. The only way to bring proceedings to a halt is to pick him up forcibly and carry him the last part of the way home. He will be whining and struggling all the time to get down and race back to the last hole.

For the less fortunate people who live in more urban areas, a race around the golf course or recreation ground after a ball will have to suffice. These dogs will probably need less food that the country dogs.

Jack Russells will follow a horse or a bicycle and can be very happy racing about the seashore. I knew one terrier who would spend hours running in and out of the sea catching the flat stones that his owner was making 'jump' on the water.

6 Training the Jack Russell Terrier

While it is necessary for the Jack Russell required for working to need all the particular characteristics of that very specialised sort of hunting which involves digging and burrowing into the earth, those self-same attributes are reprehensible in the house pet and close companion.

Imagine the following which could easily happen if the terrier is not trained in time:

Whilst visiting a garden proud relation, the young hopeful, instead of just relieving himself outside as was intended, had seized the opportunity to dig a trench and deep excavation in order to burrow under the pet rabbit's run, desecrating the immaculate lawn as he did so and then, with the air of a famed conjuror bringing off his most skilful trick, he deposited the inert body of the favourite rabbit on the sitting-room carpet. He didn't understand why his best trick was received with such horror. It was difficult for a little terrier, whose ancestors probably hunted the wild crags of Exmoor and whose immediate forebears probably flushed rats and rabbits from their hiding places and maybe even went down earths after foxes, to understand why his beloved mistress whom he adored above all others should beat him angrily, and why the others seemed hysterical, when all he did was present that little creature all bundled up in white and which looked something like the rat he had caught the week before.

Now the Master was saying, 'He'll have to go' which was the signal for the little dog to be sent away from everybody he knew and loved and wait in a dogs' home for a new owner. As he was not by way of being a pedigree dog, some of the more snobbish owners-to-be, on the look-out for an expensive dog to buy cheaply, overlooked him and, in the end, he was claimed by a family with young children who lived in a council flat. There was no garden to speak of – only a big open space of grass with a notice on it that no dogs were allowed. Although the family were kind and seemed fond of him and fed him and gave him a comfortable bed in the kitchen, it was so different to the happy life he had once known, and this mistress was not the same as the one in whose home he had grown up. It is easy to see, if you understand dogs – and Jack Russells in particular – why every time he got the chance, he ran off. He was looking for his previous mistress and the happy life he had once known and wanted to find again.

It is difficult but not impossible to turn the Jack Russell from a hunting dog into a well-behaved house pet. It would take years and years of breeding from non-hunting types and doubling up on these certain docile, tractable terriers before it would be possible to get enough little dogs that look like a Jack Russell but which behave like a lap-dog, such as a Pug or a Chihuahua or some other 'non-sporting' sort.

My suggestion is that if you want a lap-dog, buy a Pug or Chihuahua and forget the Jack Russell who will be much happier left to his own devices and his own special way of living. The biggest argument these prospective owners will put up is that Pugs and Chihuahuas cost a great deal of money and the Jack Russells suit their pockets much better. My answer to this is that the breeders of high-class pedigree show and breeding specimens of all sorts often get some dogs that don't come up to the standard required for these purposes but which will make someone a very happy pet. They are well-bred for temperament and health purposes but perhaps have the wrong coat or colour, or have teeth that don't meet the high standard set for them, or have the wrong ear or tail carriage. None of these factors have any derogatory effect on the dog as a pet; the price asked will be no more than would be expected for a Jack Russell and the end result will be happier by far.

If, as so often happens, the owner of a Jack Russell is fond enough of him not to wish to get rid of him despite any questionable behaviour like the rabbit affair, I may be able to suggest a compromise that will make it possible to keep the little dog. By this, I mean that the owner must be prepared to set aside the time to train the terrier how to behave in the house and garden as well as while walking in the street without him necessarily losing the will to hunt when he is in the right place for it.

I won't pretend this will be easy because the Jack Russell has mostly been able to follow his instincts and is apt to go off on his own unless any restrictions are put on him. When he is first kept in, he could get quite stubborn and misbehave in the house, biting and snapping at his owners and behaving in all sorts of other odd ways quite out of keeping with his normal character.

However, if he is an intelligent dog and mostly a very loving one too, and if the brains he needs to do his work well are harnessed to his affection for his master or mistress and if the whole training business can be carried out as a game with endless patience expended by the owner and lots of praise meted out to him, the result will be of the greatest benefit to everyone.

The first thing a dog should learn is its own name. Once he

H. M. King George V teaching his terrier to beg.

understands that his special name belongs to him alone, he will respond more quickly. A shout of 'Jack, no' will have a far more immediate effect than just a mere 'No', and the same applies to 'Jack, come' etc.

A dog senses with his nose as well as with his eyes, and the terrier is very well equipped with this sense of smell. He will recognise his master and family as much by smell as by sight. The memory of smells is strong, so he follows his master by smell and soon becomes very affectionate towards him.

House-training

From a very early age, the Jack Russell puppy should be taught to be clean in the house. If the puppy was born in the house and the mother and her litter managed properly (see page 140), the puppy will be paper-broken as soon as he is old enough to walk. I give my bitches a bed with an opening in one side. The bed should have a cotton sheet for bedding – for small puppies, J-clothes are cheap and easy to keep washed. A good place for the bed is in a play-pen with the floor of the pen lined with lots of newspaper. It will be found that tiny puppies will struggle from the nest and go out to use the paper for the proper purposes. This shows the superiority of the baby puppy over the human baby. The human takes the best part of a year to learn to control himself and wets and messes as and where he wants. If the puppy is given access to a wad of newspaper, he will use it from the very beginning and will usually hold himself until he gets to it. The newspaper can be put on a tray and moved about and the pup will still find it, especially if he has used it from the begininng.

If this same tray is placed behind the door through which the pup is later expected to go through into the garden, he will use it and then when he is old enough to go outside, the tray should be put out with him. It will be familiar to him and he should automatically use it. The first hurdle will be over when the puppy goes to the door to look for his tray of newspaper before wetting or messing. If he doesn't find it, he will use any other paper he finds – letters, wrapping paper etc. The main thing is that he must find what he is looking for and then he will use it. If, however, it isn't there or he can't get out and look for it and there is no other suitable place handy, he will use the most comfortable place – the long fur rug in front of the fire, perhaps, which will resemble the long grass and be nice to stand on! It is the owner's fault if the puppy can't find a suitable place where and when he wants it. There is little use in punishing the puppy when he makes a pool or mess in the house if he has not been given the chance to do it outside or on the tray.

The best system is strict daily, even hourly, routine to start with. Every hour on the hour put the puppy outside where it should be encouraged to spend a penny. If he doesn't seem to understand, put a piece of paper he has already used under a brick outside the back door. Place it under the over-hang of the roof so that he can be popped out in the most severe weather and train him with the words 'Be quick' or 'Hurry up'.

My dogs go out to the tune of 'All dogs out' and when we think they have been out long enough we open the door and call 'All dogs in'. This works in the car and in strange places as it is telling the dogs what we expect of them and as they know that in a short time they are going to be called in again they hurry to perform as soon as they are let out.

When there are older dogs already in the house, they teach the younger ones. Most of my bitches will take their young out and show them what to do.

When there is only one puppy and the owner is new to puppy training, it is as well to bear in mind that the pup will wet the moment he wakes and within a very short time of eating or drinking – in fact, it is nearly a reflex action. Any excitement or fright will also have the same effect. So put the puppy out on waking and immediately after his meals. It is not wise to put drinking water down for the puppy at night.

He won't sleep the night through and if, when he wakes, he finds himself on his own with nothing to do, he will drink water out of boredom. Then he won't be able to wait till morning and will make a puddle. He can drink all he needs during the day when there is somebody handy to pop him outside.

This quite difficult task of training a young puppy to be house-clean can take anything up to a month of constant supervision before he may be quite reliable, but I have known them get perfectly clean after a few days if constant watch is kept on them and they are always taken through the same door and to the same spot to do their puddles on. Always lavish words of praise when he performs in the right place.

Difficulty often arises if he leaves his place of birth and goes to his new home where he has to learn all the new doors, voices and signals etc. He won't have his mother about to lick him clean and to encourage him to pass his urine and excretia with her usual vigorous tongue massage.

Until a puppy knows his way round, he should be carried to the place set aside for him. When he wets on the newspaper, this should be left there until the next time he needs to go. When he smells it, he will recognise that he has been there before without causing any trouble and should oblige again and again. Expensive puppy trainers are only smelly chemicals that remind the dog of their purpose and his own smell is cheaper and more effective. No harsh words should be used but much praise should be given and always use the same words like 'That's a clean boy'. The chief thing is not to wait for him to misbehave in the house and then to punish him, but to forestall him and get the going outside so connected in his mind with being clean that it shouldn't occur to him to mess indoors.

If it is found that the puppy is clean in the day-time but still cannot last through the night, it is a good idea to put him in a travelling box with a wire door, and on a blanket. He won't want to soil his blanket and will try to wait until you let him out in the early morning. It is a kindness to get up extra early during this part of his training so his little bladder isn't strained too much. A kind approach, patience and understanding usually result in a clean house dog.

Obedience training should start as a game and must not last too long or it may put too much strain on a young and sensitive dog. It must be borne in mind that the dog will only understand 'No' or 'Yes' at first and whether his master is pleased or displeased. The dog will only understand the difference if the tone for those two words is always the same – pleased and smiling for 'Yes' and displeased and frowning for 'No'. If the pleased 'Yes' is accompanied by a pat – sometimes a small reward – the lesson will be learned that much quicker. One of the dog's main delights in living is eating, and it is sometimes a good idea to give training on an empty stomach. When the lesson is over and well-performed, praise him highly and give him his food. Even lead training, which is often irritating to a gay, boisterous puppy when it is first started, will be tolerated far more willingly if it is always followed by his meal. This routine will have to be repeated often before the dog realises the connection but, given sufficient time, he will understand. When he does connect the two, the biggest battle will have been won and the dog should become eager and willing to have his lead put on because he knows that his meal will follow his lesson.

The Sit

To teach the Sit, press down on the dog's hindquarters firmly and quickly with the left hand, and with the right hold his front paws on the ground a little way behind where his front feet would be standing. Alternatively, press under his throat and push back his muzzle saying 'Sit'. Praise him when he is sitting down on his haunches and repeat this exercise every day several times. Never ask the dog to do this exercise too often since he will become bored; it should always be performed in the spirit of enjoyment so that the puppy feels he is being very clever when you praise him.

The Down

Going from the Sit to the Down is more difficult. Get the dog on your left side, just a little way behind you so that he can see you all the time. Hold him by his collar or by the back of the neck with one hand and with the other press down on his rump, then pull his front feet forward still pressing on his rump and repeating the Down command each time you press. After a time – and this will vary with the individual dog – he will get the idea and lie down of his own accord. It is a good idea if a stake has to be used during the training period and when staking out while working to use two stakes and cross them over each other before looping the training cord round it. It won't tangle, twist or stop the dog from freely running round the stake.

Walking on the Lead

Once his basic house-training has proved successful, the next lesson may be walking on a lead. The younger this is attempted, even at ten weeks old, the easier it will be. The first collar should be a very soft affair and mustn't be too tight. Buy it big enough to allow for growth and get an extra hole bored in it for a better fit at the start. It should be loose round his neck but too tight to slip over his head. A choke chain will be quite unnecessary and is not something I ever advocate, as it teaches by pain.

Once the collar is accepted – it should be put on just before playtime and the dog sent chasing a ball or chewing a large bone, anything in fact that will absorb his attention – he will hardly notice he is wearing it at all.

Start lead training by letting him run about with a piece of thin cord hanging from the collar. Everytime it touches his body when he is running about, he will be conscious of it but as it won't impede him in any way or restrict him, he will probably ignore it. After a while, pick up the end of the cord and he will probably object and pull if he feels you holding on to it. He will pull in the opposite direction to your pulling, so the object is not to let him feel you have the end, but to let him lead you where he wants and he will soon accept the attachment to his collar.

The fight will start when you want him to go in the direction *you* wish. If he hangs back, just keep on walking, while talking gently to him. Don't let a scolding voice put him off. If he hesitates, don't let him sit down to be dragged along but pull him forward, moving swiftly all the time. At intervals, give the lead a tug in an upward direction so that his four feet leave the ground and, as he lands, he will have to keep his feet moving to try to regain his balance. There are the moments when he must put his feet down and keep them moving; he should be praised for his clever walking and the lead will be used as an aid to his balance. This so-called propulsion is really all that is needed and he will soon discover that he gets along better than when he is hanging back. Never keep the lesson up for too long and end it with lots of praise and then his dinner so that he connects the lead-walking with something enjoyable. Do the same thing in the same way and at the same time every day until he walks easily at your side and you then know you have won another battle.

An annoying trait and the sign of a badly-trained dog is one that pulls forward and nearly wrenches your arm out. Correct this by teaching the dog to 'heel, i.e. walk at your side with his head slightly in front of your left leg. Note that heeling should always be on the *left* side of the handler and the lead should be held in both hands to teach this exercise. The left hand should hold the lead close to the collar and the right hand should hold the loop of the lead, or twist the lead firmly round the right hand to anchor it. Always keep the palm facing downwards and use the left hand to guide the dog. If the dog is in a sitting position to start, say 'Keep to heel' and walk forward at the same time. Before he can pull forward, stop and say 'Sit'. Then walk forward again saying 'Keep to heel' and stop every few yards with the word 'Sit'. Keep talking to him and make him look up to you. If he pulls too far forward he won't be able to see your face. If he does get too far forward as though he is taking you for a walk, use both hands and pull on the lead, jerking him back sharply enough to lift him off the ground and carry him back as far behind you as possible, but making sure he always lands safely on his four feet. Repeat this every time he pulls forward so that he will gradually understand that he must walk *beside* you and not in front.

If he proves very difficult to train in this respect, another method is to walk him close to a wall and every time he pulls forward tap him on the nose with a rolled-up newspaper held in the right hand. But this way, you do not have nearly so much control over the dog and he won't learn that walking close to heel is more companionable and, therefore, more enjoyable for both dog and handler. Fear is never a good basis for getting him to obey and is merely the line of least resistance.

Coming to Heel
This is probably the most important lesson of all, and a dog which responds immediately shows that it has been well-trained and will probably carry out all his other lessons well. Always use his name when you call him – 'Jack, heel'.

When you start this lesson, ask him to sit, then move a few yards away from him and then call him. He should come to you automatically because he wants to be with you. It is a good idea to teach him this lesson when there isn't anything else about to distract him; you should also keep the early lessons short, otherwise he will become bored which is the last thing you want. Continue the lesson by moving further away from him each time, then carrying out the same procedure: calling him by name and then, when he reaches you, asking him to sit.

When he responds to your call from several yards – and this may take a week or so depending on the dog – try calling him when he is not expecting it. Call him when he is snuffling round the garden perhaps. He will probably turn to look at you and you should then repeat the call, 'Jack, heel' and, all being well, he will come to you. Don't forget to give him plenty of praise.

If your puppy seems reluctant to come to your call, you can try tempting him with little bits of liver or biscuit, but don't do this unless it is necessary. He will soon come if he knows you have a tit-bit for him, so after a couple of calls, don't give him anything and then he won't come to expect it.

If your dog refuses – at any age – to come to heel because he is busy doing something else, be firm. Calling him all the time, go to fetch him, put him on the lead and, scolding him, take him to the place from where you called him.

So many accidents can be avoided by an obedient dog, so never call him to heel without a good reason. If you do, he may not bother to trust you when it really matters.

The Stay

The Stay is another important lesson and one of the most difficult for the little active wandering terrier to learn. If he can learn it, it will make all the difference to the lives of the people who own him. It should be taught when the dog is still young.

Take two crossed metal stakes as described, put them through the loop of the lead and peg them firmly in the ground, making sure that the lead has a swivel clip to prevent him from choking himself. Put the dog in the Down position and keep walking round him, repeating 'Stay'. Walk away from the dog and then round in circles and step over him a few times repeating 'Stay' all the time. Let the dog stay 'staked-out' for five to ten minutes a day for about a week while you make larger and larger circles round him. If he gets up from his Down position place him back in it with the correct firm words.

The next stage is to make him think that his lead is attached to the stake but in fact, lie the loose lead beside the stake. Then continue your circling, walking further away all the time. Finally, place him alone in the Down position, tell him to 'Stay' and then walk away from him. If he has assimilated all the earlier lessons, he should remain where he is until you tell him to 'Come'. Make sure he does come to you and doesn't dash off to the nearest hedgerow. Lavish praise on him.

If a Jack Russell doesn't receive some ordinary basic training by about the time he is four months old, it will be very difficult to get him to co-operate at a later stage, as he won't take kindly to the idea at all.

Walking on the lead, sitting, coming to heel and staying down while the handler is out of sight are the most useful things to teach him. The Stay is very important and if properly taught it will certainly make life easier when shopping, as he should be quite trustworthy enough to be left outside a shop for as long as his owner needs to be inside. This is really out of character with the Jack Russell whose instinct it is to get easily bored by waiting and go off on his own, so very careful training must be given.

If more obedience training is needed, attendance at a training school or the study of specialist books on the subject are the best ways of gaining more knowledge. Training schools are held in most areas and the post office, police station or Citizens' Advice Bureau in the town where you live will furnish all the necessary information. There is nothing to beat practical experience but, if this is not possible, you cannot do better than study Barbara Woodhouse's methods in her very useful book *Dog Training My Way*.

Tom Scott, one of the original police dog handlers, has his own training school for dogs and handlers since he retired from the Police Force. His fees for this obedience training course are expensive but his

The author's three month old puppy Gilly can retrieve a ball.

methods are effective, as I saw when I visited him at his training ground at the Metropolitan Water Board's ground near Hampton. However, if it is found necessary to have a Jack Russell trained by a professional, it would only be necessary to teach him the ordinary basic obedience training. Some of Mr Scott's work is for Security and Police Forces which would be out of character for our small friend.

TRAINING FOR WORK

If you intend to have your puppy trained as a working terrier it is wise to wait to start this training until he is old enough and physically strong enough to cope with all the various types of rodent and predators that he is likely to come up against. Jack Russell used his terriers entirely against the fox, and others like Arthur Heinemann were more interested in badger digging and otter hunting so his terriers had to be big enough and clever enough to tackle this much more formidable foe. Fox hunting is still with us, the badger is now a 'Protected Species' and the 'otter' is very nearly one, it is only a matter of the paperwork. What work can our little labourer in the field find to do to make his life a *complete* one? Rabbiting has always been a pastime that has occupied a good many country dwellers and if taught to do his part correctly the terrier can be of great help. Nowadays rabbits have learned to live above ground since myxamatosis, that dread disease, wiped out nearly the whole population. It was only those that lived in country that was too hard to burrow into that survived so the present population of rabbits gives the terriers a much harder time than they did when men sent ferrets down the rabbit holes to drive out the unfortunate rabbits into nets or, if shooting was the order of the day to be chased away by the terriers. Sometimes terriers had to go down the hole to rouse up a ferret who had decided to make a meal of a rabbit, and sometimes terriers were used alone and not ferrets. A lot of fun was had this way too – one terrier went down a burrow to chase out the rabbit, while another remained at the entrance to catch the rabbit as it came out or to chase it into the middle of the field for the guns to get to work.

In this instance I was taught by a real expert, not to allow my dog to poke his nose in the hole in case he frightened the rabbit from coming out. It was necessary for the dog to lie to one side, where he would have a good view and near enough for him to grab the rabbit or be near it to stop it going back down.

My little Toff was a wizard at marking a hole – he never told us wrong and if we saw his tail go up and his elbows go down we knew the rabbit was there. Such a dog is worth his weight in gold for many dogs will dig a hole that they have seen a rabbit bolt into, or burrow about at the entrance to a hole but a good dog is one that knows his prey is at home when it is in the hidden recesses of an underground burrow. This was very useful in the days when rabbits lived their usual normal underground existence. Fred Hawkes, who taught me a lot about rabbiting as about many other similar pursuits, always liked a terrier a *bit on the leg* because they could run much faster after the rabbits. Toff was just such a one and a very good dog he turned out to be.

The first thing he had to learn was how to behave with the ferrets. I had had to teach Toff not to go after kittens by letting the mother cat teach him the lesson and so we let him nose at a ferret while held tightly on a lead. Expecting it to run away when he approached he was rather taken aback when the ferret held its ground and, when Toff put his nose down to it he got promptly nipped. He tried it again, got nipped again enough to make him jump up in the air. That was the end of it. He never, never went after a ferret so was able to work with them quite successfully. My ferreting days are over now but my son tells me that in order to cope with the rabbits that live above the ground it is necessary to use quite different tactics.

Training for Work in the Field

The dog has got to be steady on the 'Stay' as he will have to lie still while the hedges and ditches are being 'Beaten'. A very steady terrier can be allowed to nose his way along, through gorse and bracken in all the places the rabbits hide. It is easy to see the places that are inhabited by rabbits as they leave their droppings about. Having found a likely spot, and when you have two or three dogs available, put one in a ditch, one in the field and your tenderfoot will probably have to be staked to the ground where you want him to 'Stay'. Also he needs to be kept on a long length of line, in case he pulls up his stake and makes off after the rabbit. Dogs do too much damage to the rabbit if allowed to catch it themselves so while they are a great help in marking the place where the rabbits are, and then chasing the rabbits out of the ditch or hedgerow, they are so hard in the mouth that they kill and damage the flesh too much to use the rabbit for the table. Terriers are no good when shooting game for this reason, even though a lot of them make excellent *pointers*. When training a terrier the person responsible must give all his attention to his dog, and not work with the ferrets or the gun. Watch the dog carefully when a rabbit does come out into the open and make him sit so that he won't frighten it back out of sight. This is a very difficult lesson for a young and eager hunt terrier and if he moves after the rabbit or gives tongue and gives presence away he will spoil the sport. Keep him quiet at these times, even if it means you have to hold his jaws together to do so. Put him in the *Stay* and when he moves, if he isn't staked, you will have to jerk him back or press him firmly to the ground. He won't learn in five minutes, but if he is always taken to the same spot, told the same instructions and staked out and then released by the same person, he will in time connect the whole thing up with an enjoyable afternoon. A steady teacher will produce a steady worker. Some terriers have an instinct for the work and take to it like a duck to water, while some never seem to get the hang of it and so are best left at home. This is a Jack Russell's proper place in the order of things so he should be given the chance to follow his own intuition to see how he will shape. It may take six months for him to become really proficient but when he is properly schooled there is no end to the enjoyment you both will get out of life not to mention the fact that your larder will be the richer too.

Fox Hunting

Most hunts today have their own 'Hunt' Terriers which travel in the Huntsman's saddlebag and are called by a special note on the Master's Horn. These little dogs are trained up to the minute, know their work admirably and bolt their fox as soon as they are put down, in our part of the country. They are allowed to do their work while the hounds are taken out of the way, then when the fox is bolted the Master signals with a different note on his horn and 'Away They Go'. Sometimes followers on foot bring their terriers hoping that the Master will need them but in years they are never called for. It was different on the Moors that Parson Jack Russell hunted for that 'hollow' country and the fox had miles of subterranean tunnels to hide in needing more terriers than the hunt had provided sometimes.

It would never do for you to send your terrier down an earth without the Master's permission as he will have his own special terrier man who will know every inch of the locality.

A little Hunt Terrier is no match for a wounded fox who can be a deadly foe, so all holes are sealed and he is smoked out and shot with a humane killer, or a very wise, experienced and robust, hardy type of

Mr R. W. Maling with his terriers Sammy and Dandy and Barker and Nipper, hunt terriers of the North Northumberland Hunt.

terrier is sent down who will drive the fox out but knows how to keep its distance and, if he has to come up to the fox will be able to give a good account of himself. What he has to do is to get as close to the fox as he can then sit still and 'bay' at the fox and keep on baying until he is dug up to, if such a course proves necessary.

Jack Russell Terriers also have a great aptitude for destroying rats. I for one am thankful for this as I have a particular horror of rats and as the rat-catcher employed by our Council prefers to poison them rather than to catch them with dogs in the age-old way. They tell us that the poison they use is not harmful to dogs and cats but, I for one prefer not to have to try it out on them and so we forego the pleasure or otherwise of a visit from our 'Vermin Willy' as he is known locally. I am coward enough to be glad to have a dog at my heels to send in to any shed I need to enter, so he can frighten the rats before I need to enter. We have a little river running through our property and the dogs love to hunt for rats along the banks, as there are lots of holes and plenty of sport. Barns and stables are also good schools for a young terrier as he needs to meet plenty of rats so that he can have practice in killing expertly with a single quick nip at the back of the neck and tossing the rat over his head. When the hayricks used to be cleared our terriers would join the cats in disposing of the mice that would be harbouring there, but it must be admitted that they weren't a patch on Spats our old Mouser.

Toff's mother Decie had a very good way with rats, she would crouch by a piece of drain-pipe which led from a rat-hole in the duck-house. The rats had to stay in the bottom as the sides were too slippery, and as they made their way along she waited her time, picked her moment correctly it would seem for she always laid out a line of dead rats for us to see after her self-imposed pest destroying episodes.

If there is pain or punishment or boredom, the dog may never forget and will connect these discomforts with the idea of hunting and go stubborn and uncooperative. It has sometimes been impossible for certain people to work with particular dogs should their two temperaments be opposed to one another. In such cases it is better to pass the dog on to another trainer or let someone else do the training instead of the owner. The charge for this is high as it entails much specialised knowledge and special aptitude.

Over the years I have lived in the country and have spent much time with experts in every field. I have, luckily, picked up no end of spurious knowledge, some of which, being in the nature of old wives' tales, does not appear in books. I give some of these hints as they provide answers for some of the more vexing problems that can occur when dogs and their owners have to live as neighbours with all sorts of terrain, animals, occupations, dangers and hazards of everyday life in the country.

Country Code

It is the duty of every dog owner, and Jack Russell owners in particular, to bring up his dogs to obey the country code. This means they should never be allowed to chase chickens, sheep, cows, horses or any other farm stock. For one reason the farmer needs his stock for his living and being chased by even the smallest puppy can have a most dangerous effect on animals when they are carrying young. Also there have been hundreds of cases where an unruly puppy has run in the path of a cow, bull or horse and been tossed or trampled to death.

I once sold a puppy to some friends who were breeders of pedigree donkeys and as the pup grew up amongst them and always accompanied his owners when they were inspecting the donkeys, dog and donkeys were the best of friends. One day, the owners visited another donkey farm where the donkeys were not used to dogs. The little terrier ran among them as light-heartedly as he had done at home but, unfortunately, he was trampled to death right before his owners' eyes.

Chasing chickens has always been a favourite pastime. In the old days, we kept ours on free-range and they would run all over the place and lay their eggs in barns, sheds, under hedges and sometimes even in the manger in the stable. It used to be a game we would play – dogs *versus* children: who could find the eggs first? At the first sign of the hen leaving her nest, she would cackle in the manner all hens do, and dogs and children would make for the spot post-haste. The terriers would always bark in excitement and give their presence away and were then called off. Our poodles, on the other hand, went quietly about it and would lift up the egg very gently and carry it off. We even taught the poodles to collect the eggs by putting their noses under the hens before they had left the nest! Their soft mouths hardly ever broke one. If the Jack Russells got it, the egg broke as soon as the sharp teeth touched it. When eggs got very expensive, the chickens were shut in wire runs and some good fun was lost. My youngest daughter had got some bantams and had them running loose, so the dogs had to be trained not to chase them, but I am sure a lot of egg stealing must have gone on because my dogs always had good shiny coats – a sure sign that raw eggs are part of the diet.

Sometimes a Jack Russell, or any other dog for that matter, will turn chicken- or duck-killer and then he is a serious menace. It is very difficult to train an older dog out of these bad habits, so a young puppy must be trained from the start. One way is to take the puppy out on a long lead and walk him among a flock of chickens and as soon as he moves towards one, yank him back sharply, scolding as you do so, and say 'Jack, no' in a very loud stern voice.

Jack Russell Terriers have no fear of animals larger than themselves, so here again it means careful control over young puppies by never allowing them off the lead where sheep are about. This will keep them under control, and the desire to chase sheep should not enter their minds while they are getting used to the furry bundles that scamper across the field. When the dog has learnt the primary lesson of 'Sit and Stay', it will be possible to allow him his freedom on a walk across the fields and, when his eye is caught by the sheep grazing and he looks as if he wants to go to investigate, a sharp command of 'Sit' should stop him in his tracks.

This is a valuable lesson in traffic too, and many dogs' lives have been saved by the sharp command being obeyed just when they have been attracted by a cat or perhaps another dog on the other side of the road. As a rule, they are off like lightning so, if the owner is foolish enough to have the dog out without its lead on, it is essential that he should have been taught to 'Sit and Stay'.

The Stay is very important to the working terrier. Full details of this lesson are given on page 94. It should be taught by the owner or handler going out of sight and the dog remaining in the Down position. He can be taught to sit there for hours guarding something, or allowed to get up after a few minutes. To get him to stay for a long time, tell him to 'Down' and then 'Stay'. This lesson takes a lot of training but, once accomplished, it will stand the dog in great stead when working or in ordinary everyday life.

Years ago, my husband used to take one of our Jack Russells out shooting. One evening I met him and the dog returning from a day's sport. I was on my way to the post office and my husband stopped me on the drive and said he would come into the village with me. He stood his gun up against the barn wall and said to the terrier, 'Look after the gun'. We returned by another drive and, being a forgetful person, my husband went straight indoors. The next morning when he went outside he was very surprised to find the terrier still 'on guard' by his gun. She had been there all night and had not even come in for her supper although she must have heard her name being called. We had just assumed she had gone off on one of her own forays and we were ashamed of our thoughlessness. She had never been taught to guard – it was just part of her natural instinct and her love for the gun and hunting.

Terriers and Guns

Not all terriers take to walking with the guns. Some, although brave as lions in other respects, are just terrified of gun-fire. This was more common during and just after the war – which is understandable. The reason why dogs associate gun-fire with death and injury is probably connected with their fear of thunder and lightning, fireworks etc.

Most serious training for working dogs doesn't take place till the dog is about one year old. This is too late to correct gun-shyness and, if a terrier lives in the country and accompanies his master when out with the gun, he will suffer real distress and may run himself into danger when bolting in panic.

When the puppy is about three months old, he should be introduced to the sound of a small calibre shot-gun fired quite a distance away from him. Some other person should fire the gun while the dog's owner holds his head, stroking him and speaking quiet words to him. On no account should the owner jump when the gun is fired, but the pup must be reassured and made a fuss of. After daily sessions of this, a larger calibre gun can be used or the small one fired a bit nearer the dog. When the dog has smelt the gun and realised that there is no reason to have any personal fear, he should be left by himself while the shot is being fired. If he stays reasonably calm, all well and good. If the dog shows signs of nervousness after several sessions, it may be a good idea to fire the gun fairly near him when he is busily engaged in his favourite sport of eating his dinner! *Never* take a newly acquired dog out with the gun and fire over his head to see if he is gun-shy. If he wasn't before you did that, he most certainly will be then. Also, you should never let a child 'shoot' his cowboy cap pistol at a puppy – or a fully-grown dog for that matter. Since you can't really blame the child for doing this as he would know no better, it is wise to banish all toy guns from the house.

It may not matter if the Jack Russell doesn't take kindly to gunfire but I maintain that a good master should try to see that his young dog is not frightened of anything, and it is a true saying that familiarity breeds contempt.

Living With A Working Terrier
A lot of women I know object to having a working terrier in the house because they say they bring in a lot of dirt from the fields, are smelly and harbour fleas, lice, ticks and harvestors, etc. My answer would be that as he has done a day's work he is entitled to a day's food and all the home comforts possible. Some of our dogs make for the stable, but mostly they like to be indoors with the family so the only thing to do is to try and make them more acceptable in the house. All our dogs are put into a paper sack of anti-insecticidal powder and shaken thoroughly – only their heads are left out. We go to work on heads and ears with a soft toothbrush rubbing the same powder well into the skin. Beds and rugs they like to lie on are washed in a solution of the powder and they don't seem to pick up harbingers – if they did there is probably enough stuff in their coats to kill off or at least make it very unpleasant to fleas and lice. For mud, earth and general dirty conditions we throw them into a half-barrel that used to contain geraniums, but is now filled with a mixture of the loose hay on the barn floor pine sawdust and straw. By the time they get to the house the dirt has gone, rubbed off by the straw, they smell good thanks to the pine sawdust and the corn starch shines their coats up so that they are sparkling. Even longer coated ones are easy to cope with this way, the cornflour doesn't come out on one's clothes or furniture or carpets. This is a trick used on show dogs if they

cannot be bathed or the weather is too cold, but an excellent cleaner all the same.

General lessons

No two dogs react in quite the same way and, while the Jack Russell is a pack dog and works quite happily in a pack, each one will be found to be a complete individual in his own right, and it is only fair that, when a puppy, he should have the undivided attention of his owner so that he can expand his personality to the full. It is during these times of early basic training that this can be dwelt upon, and once he knows that his master is pleased with him and that serious lessons are followed by a jolly romp and a lot of praise, he will soon respond enthusiastically. On no account should the lessons last for more than ten minutes at a time and, unless the puppy is very obtuse or very uncooperative, no cross words should be uttered. In fact, if one day the puppy doesn't join in with his usual alacrity, the lesson should be postponed and the puppy checked to see if he has picked up something, swallowed something or is in any way off-colour.

Except when the puppy is working round a burrow or in the hedges, it is better to keep him on a collar and lead during training periods as he is so much more under control. A showtype slip lead is quite a useful sort and can be easily slipped off during the parts of training that warrant this. No dog that goes to earth should *ever* wear a collar when he is working as it may get caught up in roots when he is underground and stop him getting out. Pieces of root could catch him behind his head through his collar where he can't possibly get at them to bite. If the collar then presses across his throat, he might be unable to give the usual bark to let people know where he is and so be choked to death in most unpleasant circumstances.

Another necessary piece of training is to stop the puppy eating wild bird's eggs and such that he may come across while he is working. Sometimes they are pheasants' eggs which are laid on the ground, and the keepers might be cross enough to shoot if they caught him at it. I have also known keepers fill hens' eggs with deadly poison to kill magpies and other birds of prey that steal pheasants' eggs. If a dog eats one of these poisoned eggs, the result would be instant death. One wishes that such selfishness in the country could be controlled, but I'm afraid a good deal of the shooting is now in the hands of syndicates made up of people seemingly ignorant of the country code and who often seem to employ the worst type of rogues to be their keepers.

The only thing for country dog owners to do is to teach their dogs not to touch or, in fact, to go near such eggs. A good way is to fill an egg shell with mustard and put it where he will find it – preferably near his food – and if he does eat it, it will usually put him off eggs for life. I only had one dog that seemed to enjoy the mustard, so we filled another shell with ipecacuanha (an emetic) and that did the trick!

What has the above training got to do with working the terrier to fox, rabbit and hare? The answer is, of course, very little, and yet every bit of advice, if carried out to the letter and instilled into your young dog from babyhood, is going to add to his value as a companion, making living with him a delight and perhaps even save his life one day. His own instinct will teach him a lot about chasing rabbits and sniffing out rats but it won't teach him not to bolt into traffic, eat poison or know the difference between chasing chickens and ducks, and chasing his natural and permitted prey. When his basic training is complete – and this can be as explained above, or can be as comprehensive as the owner likes to make it – then is the time to take him along and introduce him to those tasks for which he has been born and bred.

Rabbiting and Ratting
Chief of those tasks are rabbiting and ratting and, if he happens to have been brought up on a farm, he will quite likely have met rabbits and rats as soon as he was old enough to romp in the field. Terrier pups are full of energy even at an early age and will have been foraging around full of curiosity for some time.

It is not a good thing to let a young puppy get too near a rat before he is fairly mature as rats are terrible biters and an unsuccessful encounter can't do the puppy any good and may inflict horrible bites and damage on him. It is better to take him to watch older, steadier dogs dealing with the rat menace in their own inimitable way – one nip and tossed over the shoulder until the rats are laid out in a line. Nowadays the farms lose so much of their corn and other stores to rats that strict laws about wiring round a corn stack are in use. However, even if the old and tried happy hunting grounds are few and far between, there are still plenty of rats about and the official rat catcher is often far away in another district when he is wanted in yours.

When we were living on a farm I was only too willing to let my terrier go into the sheds and loose boxes in front of me to flush out the rats or at least frighten them out of sight before I ventured in. To feel one run across my feet would fill me with horror and I dreaded the thought of one running up my leg! When breeches or jodpurs gave way to slacks, this became quite a usual occurrence. It is a wise precaution to either tuck your trousers into your Wellingtons or tie them round the bottom tightly with binder cord. I used a pair of skiing trousers which fitted inside my boots and they were a great comfort.

There were times when we had an invasion of field mice, shrews and other little creatures that came from the corn-fields when the corn had been cut, and my Jack Russells had great sport. In the old days when the steam thresher used to come around, the terriers went wild with anticipation. I was too occupied with the added responsibility of feeding all the extra mouths and making sure, in times of shortage, that there would be enough coal to run the machines, so I had very little time to watch the dogs at work, but everybody in the district who had a likely terrier would bring it along. As the poultry-keeper-in-chief, I was duly grateful as the rats made short work of my duck eggs when they had no more corn to keep them going.

Watching rats steal duck eggs is a most absorbing pastime, despite the loss of the eggs. My duck house was brick-built with an earth floor on which we laid clean straw at regular intervals although the ducks muddied it up very soon since the house was beside the pond. The rats would burrow up through the earthen floor, roll an egg from out of the straw covering where the mother duck had hidden it, and then one rat would lie on its back and another one would roll the egg on to its stomach. The rat standing up would then catch hold of the prostrate rat's tail in its mouth and haul it and the egg down the hole and out of sight. We lost a lot of eggs before we discovered how they were disappearing, spending long periods looking through the glass window in the door of the duck house.

The terrier gave us the first clue, as every time she got the chance, she would dig like mad in the duck house and was always stinking of the peculiar smell that we found so unpleasant in the sitting-room at night when the heat of the fire dried her out. Those sitting above her got the full benefit of the ozone as it drifted up! She was the only one to grumble when a sheet of fine mesh wire netting was laid across the duck house floor to keep the rats at bay and save the eggs for market.

Although a Jack Russell can quite easily manage to kill rats before his first birthday, it is better to let him mature fully before he tackles larger prey, since rabbits, for instance, take quite a bit of carrying if he is going to get them out of the holes himself. Men often use ferrets to flush out rabbits and sometimes more than one rabbit will bolt out of a hole and then the terriers will be allowed to go after that. Not many rabbits seem to live in burrows since the outbreak of the rabbit-killing disease, myxamatosis.

Working with the Foxhounds

It must never be forgotten that the original Jack Russell Terriers were bred by Parson Jack to go after foxes. The sporting parson hunted his pack of terriers with his own pack of foxhounds all over the moors round his North Devon home. His terriers used to live in the house with him as personal friends and he was firmly of the opinion that this made them more adept in the hunting field because of their close proximity to their master. This is true of the breed today – they flourish best where they are allowed to be members of the family and join in all the family jaunts, and it never seems to have an adverse effect on their ability as workers.

To buy a trained Jack Russell Terrier all ready to take its place in the hunting field could cost several hundred pounds. Hunt servants often train them but, if they are willing to sell one, it would be as well to make sure that there isn't some very good reason for letting the terrier go.

For anyone contemplating owning one, there is far more satisfaction in buying a young, healthy puppy about eight to ten weeks old, rearing it sensibly and giving it the simple basic training already described. What is wanted is a terrier who is not too hard in the mouth or too aggressive, as the real purpose in entering a fox's earth is to 'give tongue' which enables the huntsmen or terrier man to determine his whereabouts. If he attempts to take on the fox himself, he will surely get injured and may be out of action for weeks. His job is to enable people outside the hole to decide exactly where the fox is lying so that he can be dug out and allowed to escape so that the hunt can continue.

A terrier who 'throws his tongue' is also unpopular because there is no need for him to keep barking. He must keep the fox at bay until assistance arrives.

You can take the youngster along to watch how the pack at the local kennels set about their work, but you must get permission from the Master to do this before you go. The hunt servants have more than enough to do without having to teach hordes of terriers how to work. But if they are willing to help you, both dog and owner can pick up a lot of useful training and many huntsmen will be free with all sorts of advice, especially if it is continued over a pint at the local afterwards. Never let your untried puppy off the lead at these times but, after a few sorties with the pack, take him out on your own and see if he can pick up the scent of a fox. He should be a good two-year-old before he is allowed to go down an earth after foxes as he needs to be matched in weight and quick and crafty to avoid the fox's sharp teeth. Ratting and other hunting will have helped to prepare him for this.

When you and your terrier have been accepted as regular followers of the hunt and you recognise the special sound on the huntsman's horn which means a terrier is wanted as the quarry has gone to ground, then is the time to allow your young hopeful free access to his opponent. He is almost certain to get the worst of his first encounters but as he gets more experienced, he will become more and more eager to take part in this favourite of all pastimes, as a truly bred little descendant of the Parson's famous Trump should be. Release him quietly and before letting him enter the earth, he should be held at the entrance for a moment so that he can accustom himself to the sounds and happenings down below.

When waiting to enter a terrier to earth, some handlers grasp him by the tail or the scruff of the neck. To a tough, hard-muscled little terrier it wouldn't matter a hoot how he is held but to onlookers, especially in these days of anti-blood sports and possible bad publicity, it must be seen to be right, and the best way is to use a slip-lead as they do in coursing, or grip the terrier by the shoulders until it is time to let him go. All working terrier breeds have broader feet than most to assist them in digging.

Hunting the Badger

Thankfully, a bill protecting the badger was passed by Parliament at the end of 1973. It is now absolutely against the law to dig out a badger by the means of spades or terriers. If there is a 'rogue' badger at work in the chicken runs, then official permission can be sought to kill it by humane means.

The Jack Russell Terriers were really too small in size – though not in spirit – to enter against the badger. Many dogs have been killed by badgers who have a knack of piercing the artery in the neck so that the dog dies before he can crawl back to the surface.

Joyce Stranger in her enchanting book *The Running Foxes* describes in almost living detail the pathetic end of a fifteen-year-old terrier who bravely entered a land-drain to flush out some hounds that were lost down it only to meet up with a fierce and angry badger. The fight that took place was uneven as the terrier's once-sharp teeth were too blunt to penetrate the badger's skin, and the badger got the terrier by the throat with his own very sharp teeth and punctured the jugular vein. The old terrier struggled to reach the entrance of the drain while his life-blood ebbed away and his breathing could be heard getting more and more laboured until he was within reach of his master's grasp. But he died while being drawn to safety. However, to the terrier, it was probably the best way to die – doing the job which he was born to do.

John Russell's favourite Terrier Tip, died in similar circumstances. Tip hardly missed a day's hunting for many seasons and never appeared in the least tired although often covering fifteen to twenty miles at a time. He died in the Chorley Earths having gone to ground after a fox. Russell dug up to him and the fox in half an hour, but the old dog was dead by the time he reached him, apparently from an attack of asthma; much to the great grief of his stricken master.

7 How to Breed from Your Jack Russell Terrier

If my readers expect to breed from their Jack Russell bitches just in order to make money, I would advise them here and now that there are better breeds to choose and far more money to be made from breeding, say, Bulldogs, gun dogs and toy dogs. Even breeders of these types find it hard to make ends meet as the cost of nearly everything to do with breeding has rocketed sky-high, except for the price of puppies which has stayed fairly steady. I bought a poodle puppy for breeding in 1946 and I paid £35. I now sell poodle puppies for only twice as much and the stock is improved over one hundred per cent.

Jack Russell Terriers, not being Kennel Club registered, do not reach such high prices as pedigree dogs except in the case of a really well-trained worker and then the sky's the limit if the right buyer comes along. There is a steady demand overseas for the breed. A dog with such a character and outlook is his own publicity agent. The hunts around the country have their own shows and so the demand for good-looking, as well as good-working, stock often exceeds the supply.

Barney, the Supreme Champion on Detling and Best in Show at the Jack Russell Terrier Club of East Anglia 1984. Owned by Mr and Mrs Hunt and bred by Mr and Mrs Spence.

Owners of good bitches should certainly consider breeding from them, as this is the only way the breed will survive. If the puppy factories, whose main object is to produce quantity rather than quality, are the criterion of the breed, the outlook will be anything but rosy. Fortunately there are, in most parts of the country, people who are dedicated to the breed and do all in their power to see that it survives. Money, surprisingly, is the last thing they think about, for the prices they get for their puppies would scarcely pay the astronomical food bills. They can take no account of the hours of care and attention which must go into the rearing of these puppies, but the high quality of some of the Jack Russells to be found today is proof that their efforts have not been in vain.

It cannot be denied that there are also many very poor specimens that don't deserve the name of Jack Russells. Some of them will have been bred from any old stock just because they are popular and buyers are gullible or ignorant. There is nothing I or any other writer can put down on paper that will have the slightest effect on such as these, but I can hope to educate the gullible and ignorant buyer so that he won't be satisfied with the poor quality of the stock offered by the puppy factories. Hopefully these might be forced out of business.

It is a great pity that the Breeding of Dogs Act of 1973 was so unwisely worded and formulated. It only affects owners of breeding bitches but not those who keep stud dogs for profit purposes only. Some unethical stud dog owners insist on terms which enable them to have any puppies resulting from the mating. They own a number of stud dogs and when a private individual – wishing to breed from a pet bitch – sends her for mating, they will often use just any dog which hasn't already been used that day. There is no studying of individual pedigrees – as they very often don't have any – and mothers can get mated to sons, fathers to daughters and brothers to sisters without

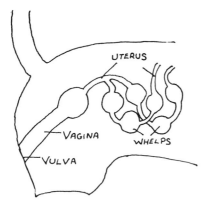
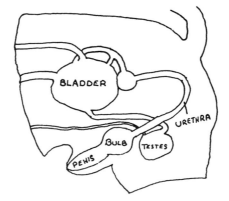

Fig. 4 Diagram of sexual organs of dog and bitch

anyone being any the wiser; in fact, without anyone caring a bit. When the puppies are ready for sale, the stud dog owner collects them and sells them quickly for quite formidable prices considering the fact that they did not have to spend money feeding the bitch and puppies. Often they do not have very creditable establishments and their customers are not given any help or guidance with their purchase. Diet sheets are expensive to produce and, in any case, many of the sellers haven't the faintest idea what a diet sheet should contain. See Chapter Four – Buying and Caring for the New Puppy – on page 65.

Unfortunately such people are quite untouched by the Act, which has been foolishly restricted to owners of more than two breeding *bitches* that produce puppies for sale.

The owner of a Jack Russell bitch may not have bought her in the first place with any idea of breeding from her, but it is surprising how many people do breed from their pet bitches. For whatever reason, we will assume that the new owner of a good quality Jack Russell bitch has decided to breed from her and just doesn't know what to do.

The Heat or Season

The first thing to be considered is the age of the bitch. The second or third season is the best time to start breeding. A bitch comes into season every six months but the first season may be delayed until she is nine months old or more, and the temperature of the weather seems to have quite a bearing on this. It is difficult for the owner of the bitch which is the only dog in the house to be sure when she first comes into season. When the first season starts, carefully note the date and enter it into a diary or onto one of the breeding charts which many dog food manufacturers give away. Then make a note for six months further on and this will be about the time the bitch next comes into season. This way, it won't come as so much of a surprise!

Seasons are heralded by a sweling of the vulva, and the bitch will be seen to be licking herself a lot. Any male dog also in the house will soon give the game away! Soon a discharge of bright red blood will be seen which will get paler as the season progresses, and the vulva will soften and pucker. If there are other bitches around, they will often ride on one another and the in-season bitch may stand quite still for this. If you take her to a stud dog though, she probably will not stand still for him. Bitches don't generally accept the dog before about the tenth or twelfth day, which are the best days for mating. If the mating takes place on the tenth day and you are not sure it has been a success, it can be done again forty-eight hours later.

Choice of Stud Dog

If a stud dog has not been decided upon in advance, it is important that a decision is made quickly as soon as the red discharge appears. Good stud dogs get very booked up and, having finally decided to breed it is disappointing to discover the dog of your choice has already been promised to another bitch on the day in question.

It is very much better, therefore, to decide on a stud dog well in advance. Then you will have plenty of opportunity to study his breeding and make advance arrangements. How to find the most suitable stud dog to use for your bitch will depend on quite a few things, and setting them down will show how important it is that you make a wise choice.

In the Jack Russell breed, there are two distinct coats – smooth and rough. Some people like one and some the other. I find no genetic pattern as to how these coats occur. Litters have some of each or they can all be roughs or all smooths. I haven't found anyone who can tell me if there is a recessive gene at work here and my own experience has not shown it either.

It would seem that two rough coats mated together are apt to produce coats which are over-heavy and which often meet with disapproval from the buyers who have moulting in mind. Smooths are neat little terriers but the lack of rough hair gives them nothing to cover up their faults with so they have to be very well formed.

If the bitch's coat is broken-looking, mate her to a good smooth and the puppies should follow the mother to a certain extent. If she is rough and you like her coat, mate her to one just like her and you will probably have several roughs in the litter. Mate her to a smooth dog, and if there is a rough coat in the litter, it will most probably be a good quality one. If this rough coat is then mated to another rough coat, they would produce more rough coats than smooth but if mated to a smooth, there will probably be an equal proportion of both.

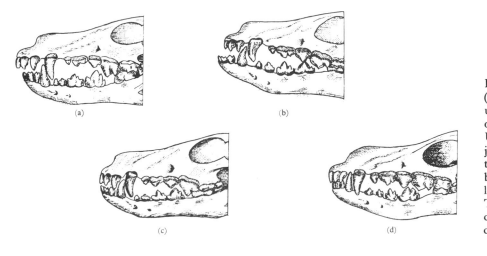

Fig. 5   The mouth: (a) Overshot. The upper jaw protudes over the lower. (b) Undershot. The lower jaw protudes beyond the upper. (c) Level bite, with upper and lower teeth meeting. This is recognised as correct. (d) Scissor bite, considered perfect

The ideal Fox Terrier and hunt terrier should be predominantly white, so don't pick a stud dog with too many markings.

It may happen that the dog you have decided upon is not available and you will be offered the use of another one of similar breeding. What decision do you make with very little time left? The first thing is to ascertain that the dog offered has a good temperament. There is absolutely no point in breeding bad-tempered Jack Russells for the pet market. Even as workers, it is not very much use having one that is too vicious to mix with other dogs.

Ask for full details of the dog's own breeding, and if you can't get to see him, ask for a photograph. Don't let him be too big as they are supposed to be of a handy size. He should have a straight front, short back and a chest which you can span with your hand. Make sure the markings are well spaced as the market is limited for splodgy ones. Ears should be dropped forward and be neat and fairly small and the teeth *must* be sound with the correct scissor bit.

Ask if the dog is 'complete' which means he has two testicles descended. This may not be important as you will not be breeding under Kennel Club regulations, but it is pointless to take the risk of producing monorchid puppies who may end up with cancer of the testicle which does not descend. Monorchid dogs sometimes have the annoying habit of being over-sexed in the most unpleasant way for a house pet and usually end up needing complete castration.

Fix on a fee and send it with the return carriage. Insist on a three-generation breeding table because even if they are all simply called Tom, Dick and Harry, at least you will be able to see how many times the same name appears and what relations are behind the dog. Ask for a receipt giving the actual date of mating so that you can work out the expected date your bitch will whelp from a gestation chart, and also ask for a signed statement that you will be allowed to repeat the mating free of cost, except for the carriage, in the event of the first one being ineffective.

The Jack Russell Dog that you choose to be the sire of your puppies must conform to a very high standard even though there are no strict rules set down by the Jack Russell Club itself.

In order to qualify as a sire under their jurisdiction, the owner of the stud dog should be made to supply a vet's certificate to the effect that the dog is free from any hereditary defects such as hip dysplasia, Patella luxation, PRA (Progressive Retinal Atrophy), cataracts or any other hereditary diseases or conditions. The English Kennel Club have several schemes whereby breeders can have their dogs tested by x-ray and other veterinary methods so that the Kennel Club are able to issue certificates to show that the relevant dog has been tested and proved to be free from these specific hereditary conditions.

Dapper, born 1950, was the foundation sire of Ted Adsett's strain. He was the Chiddingston Farmers' Hunt terrier all his life and was a wonderful worker and sire of the Sandhurst Draghounds' famous Jane who was their best worker.

The owner of the stud dog is held responsible for any hereditary failings of the litter so it would seem prudent for any owner to arm himself with veterinary proof that his stud dog is free from *all* the diseases and conditions listed on a Kennel Club certificate.

Sending your Bitch to the Stud Dog

Important advice I must give is not to use a dog from too near your own home just because of the ease and convenience of getting your bitch to him. It is much better to send her right across the country to use a proved and capable sire for your litter. In the days when Eire and Northern Ireland were able to accept such cargo by air, I sent my bitches over and also flew them up to Scotland if it was the home of the best dog available.

If your bitch is ready about the time a good dog is visiting a show in your area, you may be lucky enough to arrange things accordingly but it will be a remarkable coincidence since the difference of twenty-four hours either way can often spoil an otherwise propitious mating. If there is a good dog with a proved reputation for siring the type of puppies I hope you aim to breed, book him quickly and take your bitch to him when his owner advises, since the experience the owner has will be far greater than yours.

If you are unable to take the bitch personally and have to send her instead, it is quite a simple matter provided you know the ropes and take the trouble to attend to the little details which make all the difference to her arriving promptly at a reasonable hour and being collected as soon as possible when she arrives. Never guess the station and address but find out in advance together with the time of the train and the amount of time you have to have her there beforehand.

Obtain a strong travelling box with a sturdy, very thickly-wired door with a strong fastening. If a padlock is used, wire the key to the handle. String can sometimes break and then the key will be lost. The box should be the right size for your bitch. If you send your little terrier off in a converted tea-chest, she will be thrown all over the place every time the box moves. The right size should give her room to stand up comfortably. It should be fairly narrow so that she won't fall over if she is standing up and the box lurches, but deep enough for her to turn round if she needs to.

I always put a label addressed back to me in an envelope with holes bored in it for the string to be pulled through. On the outside of the envelope, I *print* the name of the people and the station she is going to and also put their telephone number on it so that they can be informed of her arrival, and come to collect her at once. If you put the address on the box itself, she may get loaded on a lorry for delivery and this we do not want. Tell the goods office clerk that she is TO BE COLLECTED at such and such a Station. Give the time of the train and ascertain its arrival time at her destination. Then you should telephone the owner of the stud dog to say that the bitch is on her way and will arrive at such and such a time. Tell them to take off the envelope and expose the label inside which you addressed back to your home station and you will know that the box will be correctly labelled for the bitch's return. Don't forget to put your telephone number on the label so that you can be informed of her arrival.

Perhaps you think I have gone into too much detail over this procedure, but you would understand if you had ever experienced the frustration of having dog boxes put off trains at the wrong station, not put on trains they were intended for as the labels had fallen off, got lost or were too wet to read, or other unexpected happenings that can upset your most well-laid arrangements. The awful feeling when you pick up the telephone receiver late in the evening hoping to hear that your bitch has arrived safely after you had sent her off early that morning, only to hear that although they had met every train she hadn't been found, has to be experienced to be understood.

This happened once when my bitch had to change trains from Waterloo to King's Cross to go on up to York. She had been transported across London to King's Cross but had not been seen since. I frantically telephoned everybody I could think of, but in vain, so I made the journey by car in speedway time and after getting everyone then available at that late hour to help in my search, I asked to have the time checked when she arrived, so that I could take up the matter with Waterloo. They unlocked the Goods Office and while they were looking for a time sheet I must have spoken and my bitch recognised my voice, for suddenly there was the most unholy shriek of joy and a great scrabbling noise. We found her box behind some crates of bicycles. The 'Livestock' label had fallen off and her box had been treated as an ordinary piece of goods about which there was no haste.

Nowadays labels are stuck on the boxes with very strong glue and big 'Livestock' labels are put on the exposed sides of the box. I got this information from the manager of the Goods Department for British Rail and I now follow his instructions to the letter. Over many years I have had excellent associations with the railway. On one very dreadful occasion I was being sent a bitch and when she failed to arrive I couldn't track down her owner. Knowing how my own bitch had been lost, I got in touch with every station master between our two stations but there was no news at all. In the end, I rang the police at the other end, discovered that my friend had had an accident on the way to the station and that she was in hospital and the bitch had been taken over by the R.S.P.C.A.!

In all cases it is better to take your bitch to the dog yourself if at all possible. It is not usual for the dog to visit the bitch.

Condition of the Brood Bitch

A bitch should be mated only if she is in the peak of condition. It will be hard enough for a well-nourished and healthy bitch to whelp and rear a good litter, but it is foolish to attempt it if she is out of condition and not one hundred percent. Don't think that having a litter is going to improve a bitch's health. On the contrary, it is going to put an added strain on it. The answer is simple – do all you can to get the bitch in top form *before the mating*.

First dose her for round worms. These are quite easy to get rid of and, as long as the dose is repeated a week later, she should be clear of them for a while. Even so, the chances are that her puppies will be full of round worms and have to be dosed themselves as soon as they are old enough.

The bitch's skin must be clean and free from parasites and she may need treatment and several baths at close intervals using the particular remedies sold for the purpose. Hair around the vulva should be removed and her back parts kept washed with mild soap and warm water. Never use disinfectant or any of the 'Keep-Away' preparations sold for bitches in season as these will be equally efficient in keeping the paid stud dog at bay.

A modern version of Trump and an excellent example of the Parson Jack Russell Terrier standard. Hard coated, keen alert expression, straight-front, short-backed. This is the sort to breed.

The Mating

If the stud dog owner is short-handed and you are accompanying your bitch, you may be asked to hold your dog while the mating takes place. Grasp her shoulders, keeping her head between your hands. Just holding her head won't stop her twisting out of your grasp.

Before attempting to mate the two together, they should be allowed to play together. If there is any tendency to snap, it may turn out that she is still too early and the dog owners may offer to keep her for a few days. This should not entail any extra cost as it is as much to the stud owner's advantage as to yours that the mating should be productive. If all the signs are right and they still don't seem to 'take' to each other, it may be necessary to tape a muzzle on the most aggressive one – even on both of them – and force the mating, but this rarely happens. Never mate if either or both have full stomachs following a meal.

A good stud dog is worth his weight in gold and every care should be taken to ensure that he comes to no harm during the mating process. If wisely trained, he will allow himself to be helped and this saves a lot of time and patience. If he insists on doing the job without help, you can only try to steady the bitch and hope he strikes the right place. When sizes are assorted, this can prove a problem and sometimes it is necessary to raise the dog or bitch according to which is in need of it. When the dog's penis enters the bitch's vulva, he will work his back legs spasmodically until he gets an erection and then he will work his back legs much more vigorously and start to eject the spermatozoa inside the bitch. At this time the bulbous part at the base of the penis swells up and, when it comes in contact with the hard muscle inside the bitch's vagina, it causes a sort of violent reflex during which the penis becomes engorged with trapped blood because a valve has cut off the blood flow. The bulbous part swells up and hardens and this causes the 'tie' so that the dog and bitch are unable to part for some considerable time. This is Nature's clever way to make sure that all the ova or eggs that can be reached are properly fertilised.

After the mating, both dogs should be allowed to rest. The bitch should not be allowed to relieve herself within two hours of the mating, so every inducement should be made to get her to empty her bladder and bowels before the mating. After the mating, the bitch will still want to be kept from other dogs as she will remain attractive to them until the end of her season. The stud dog should also be allowed to rest. He should never serve two bitches in one day.

If breeding is going to be a regular practice, it is necessary to understand the mechanics of the situation right from the start. How important this is can be seen from the following entirely true story.

Some years ago I sold a pair of youngsters to a lady who lived in the more remote part of Cornwall and needed them for company. They were not sold with any ideas for breeding but she thought that by mixing the sexes, they would live amicably together. One night, I was woken by the telephone ringing at about three a.m., a very alarming time for anyone who has children abroad and cattle in off-lying fields. At the other end of the line was my friend from Cornwall, almost incoherent. She had gone to bed as usual with her little terriers sleeping on the bottom of her bed. She was disturbed by violent motion and woke to find the bitch stuck to the other by some sort of 'piece of rope'. She had gone for a kitchen knife and was about to try to cut it, but didn't know how to go about it. Fortunately for the poor little creatures, she had thought to telephone me before using it and, at that early hour with the horror of what might have been, I had to tell her about the 'birds and the bees' or as much as they concerned reproduction in dogs! If she reads this, she won't mind my writing it as she was much more horrified even than I when she realised the enormity of her intended action.

Care of the Bitch during Pregnancy

The normal gestation period is sixty-three days from the day of mating but it can range between the fifty-eighth day and the sixty-eighth day. For the first month, treat the bitch as normal. A slight change in her eating habits may occur, but nothing of significance. During the last five weeks, I like to give a special diet to enable the bitch to succour the puppies growing inside her and to nourish her in preparation for the coming confinement. At this stage, the pups are like peas on a string – the string being the blood vessel that attaches the developing puppies to their mother. This blood vessel will carry all the nourishment and as the embryo grows, the mother will need more food which should be given as two or three moderate feeds through the day, rather than one big one.

A short-legged bitch has a very uncomfortable time when carrying a litter as if she is not careful the unborn pups are banging against the ground when she is going up or down steps. If there are a lot of puppies weighing a poor little mother down it will be easy to see the advantages of breeding Jack Russells with legs long enough to enable the mother to carry her pups without the discomfort of banging her pups against everything she moves over. You feel as though you would like to put some sort of sling underneath them to keep them out of harm's way. Mate your short-legged bitches to dogs with longer legs and only keep those puppies that take after their sire, do this every time you mate your bitches and dispose of the short-legged ones 'not to be bred from' or have them spayed. They are not true Jack Russells but 'mistakes' which have been present ever since those early days when a puppy that had long legs went as a show dog and the litter mates with short legs went to the Hunt Kennels as a worker.

Breeders of working terriers who are sold on 'working' to the exclusion of 'looks' are wholly responsible for these little misfortunes. How often do you find that those breeders of the 'true' Jack Russell bemoaning the fact that indiscriminate breeders are mating their beautiful Jack Russells to short legged mongrels and so ruining their wonderful breed, when all the time they themselves are totally responsible because breeding only for working capabilities and the courage and vigour to stand up to every foe. Whereas John Russell himself had Old Jock in his sight and his first terrier the inimitable Trump to show him what good construction looked like. The breeders who came after him had no such picture in their minds and so they produced their splendid little workers breeding merely for brains and courage, with every sort of crippling device in the book – to start with they are 'dwarves' of the worst make and shape. They knew John Russell preferred his on the small side so, not wishing to learn how to produce similar types as a breeder wishing to produce show stock would have to they bred two together and produced short legs. The same size bodies but short legs. They told themselves that only the working aptitudes mattered and went on breeding from their dwarves and being completely ignorant of correct conformation and not in the least interested in anything but hunting otters and foxes, badgers and other vermin, they had to get stronger and more robust terriers to be able to cope and their choice in breeding stock was so reprehensible that they have gone completely against Nature and ended with the kind of freaks that should make them ashamed to consider asking the Kennel Club to accept them as a 'Breed'.

What they have ended up with in many cases are full sized fox terriers on little stumpy legs. In order to compensate for this imbalance Nature has given them very long couplings which are very ugly and make action very unsound, this isn't helped by a tendency to upright shoulders which in a breed with enough leg can often be overcome so action isn't affected, but on short legs this doesn't happen with the result that front action is nearly always bad. This then affects hind action which in many cases is straight in the stifle. One bitch is credited with having more Best of Breeds than any other bitch and is Supreme Champion but she is so straight in the stifle that her stifle cord could easily slip off altogether and completely cripple her. As it is hereditary any of her offspring could be the same.

It is hard to see how such breeding can be discouraged when there is no blueprint for them to conform to and Jack Russell breeders are really getting the best of both worlds at the moment because they are able to command prices of £45 or more for their pups straight out of the nest and they don't need to supply any pedigree or papers or register the puppy in any way in order to sell them as the breeders of Kennel Club pedigreed dogs have to do.

Although there is now a Jack Russell Club it has no jurisdiction over its members and no way of making them breed to a pattern in order to improve the shape and looks of this little terrier. Most of the officials are content with a rather indifferent type and are only anxious to keep it a working terrier even if it has not got legs to work with. It is easy to see why they don't wish to bother to get the Jack Russell a registered pedigree breed at the Kennel Club where they would of course need to comply with the very high standards laid down by that body for the dogs exhibited under its auspices, when they are able to show their terriers in a filthy dirty state with mud all over them and with hard lumps of neglected coat and harder lumps of mud in their poor feet and still be judged Supreme Champion.

I can only advise my readers to study the skeleton of a dog and learn a bit about balance. Find out how each bone is fitted into the next one. Study how much leg is needed in order to square off the whole outline – from the withers to the ground and from the withers to the root of the tail is 'square' and that was the shape of John Russell terriers. Miss Ellis had her terriers direct from the Parson and lost length of leg in a few generations because she was not conscious of them, I expect. On the other hand Arthur Heinemann is credited with retaining the blood of the true Jack Russell because he managed to breed them 'up on the leg' and is much admired as a result. It is easy to see how this came about as Heinemann was a well-educated man, knew about construction and, because we know he often judged at Crufts and other beauty shows we must realise that he had an eye for conformation and bred his terriers accordingly because that was how he liked them.

Somebody took him literally and bred for work again without having the 'eye' and short legs came back and stayed.

The only way to deal with this fault is to either spay all short legged bitches and castrate all short legged dogs or not to breed them or allow stud dogs to mate any bitch with short legs or who is come down from known short legs. Pedigrees will need to be given and the length of leg put against all the entries.

Nutrition

I used to add a wide variety of vitamins, calcium, cod liver oil and halibut oil and all sorts of other supplements the books and advertisements tell us a prospective mother must have. Nowadays, thanks to the extra money available for research into this field, there is a most excellent preparation known as SA 37 which is a nutritional supplement for dogs made by Intervet Laboratories, Milton Road, Cambridge. This product contains every known additive a dog's constitution requires in the correct proportion. I give my breeding stock a half teaspoon of this every day when they are not being used for breeding, but before I mate the bitches I give a teaspoon daily according to weight for a few weeks and continue this amount right through the pregnancy, lactation and weaning period and for at least two months afterwards. I therefore avoid any tendency in my bitches towards any of the deficiencies and unbalanced conditions that can affect them at such times of stress. I can say with all honesty that they have been free of any form of deficiency. In fact, when the bitches have finished with a litter, they are in just as good condition as when they started.

One thing I have proved though is that in cases where a bitch has not 'taken' after she has mated, if I give a course of Vitamin E before mating this has proved most effective in producing a live litter at the next mating. This is now common practice for the treatment of bitches who are poor breeders. A daily dose of wheat germ oil according to weight, put on one of her feeds will be an easy way of giving this Vitamin and can be obtained from any good chemist. Wheat germ in powder form can also be used according to weight, a daily dose should be worked out and given on food.

Jack Russells don't usually have more than four or five puppies, so it is not necessary to prepare for supplementary feeding and foster mothers in case the litter contains a large number. If the bitch has been chosen specifically for breeding, her pelvic measurement should be checked as this is one of the most important factors in a trouble-free whelping. If you decide to breed from her after you have had her for some time, there is consolation in the fact that Jack Russell puppies have narrow skulls and the bitches have sturdy bodies, with plenty of heartroom and good spring of rib which extends down to the hips. When the hip joints are wide apart, the pelvis is wide enough for there to be plenty of room for the puppies to pass down the horns of the uterus, which is the passage they have to pass along in order to be born.

Jack Russells are normally very active little dogs, and bitches in the early stages of pregnancy need not have their exercise reduced in any way. Jumping down from chairs should be discouraged as this could dislodge the puppies and cause an early abortion. Towards the end of her time, the bitch must have regular and sensible exercise several times a day without being allowed to tire. As she will be eating far more than usual, she will make superfluous fat if it isn't used up in energy. A fat bitch tends to behave sluggishly when giving birth but Jack Russells are probably among the least likely bitches to suffer in this way. However, it is as well for those breeding from an older bitch, who may have put on weight with her years, to be extra careful not to let her get too fat.

Such 'exertion' as a severe fight will cause shock and this could kill some or all of the puppies, depending on their position in the uterus. The ones low down will probably die at the time of the shock – those farther up may survive because they have more protection, but a dead puppy left for any length of time in the womb will decay and infect the others. It could result in all dead pups, or the survivors will be so badly affected by the contact with the dead foetus that they will be impaired physically and may even die at birth or soon after.

Towards the end of her gestation period, prepare the whelping box. It is a good idea to place it inside some form of safety area, such as a child's playpen or a wire run. Wooden whelping boxes specially designed can be bought, or you can make one. As the size for the Jack Russell is so small, the bitch will do very well in a strong grocer's cardboard box with one side cut half way down. If this is lined with a thick layer of newspaper, she will have plenty of scope for the digging and tearing she will do. If the paper is shredded for her, she won't get the same satisfaction, for the tearing-up process is part of her labour pains.

As has been said before, the gestation period is usually sixty-three days but will vary according to the size of the litter. A sizeable litter of four or five tends to arrive early, whereas one or two fat pups are inclined to hang back and be slow about making their appearance.

However, there is no hard and fast rule and it is better to be ready too early than be caught napping by an unexpectedly early whelping.

For the last few weeks, the bitch's diet should contain daily milk feeds fortified with Farex, Complan or Casilan with added glucose. An egg yolk will enrich this but it is wiser with the high price to save this extra until the pups arrive and she will benefit more from the extra nourishment. Eggs are best given raw, beaten up in one of the milk feeds. Raw meat is necessary each day – 4 to 6oz. daily split up into two feeds. Only if the litter is very large will she require more than this. Nursing mothers whose milk is slow in coming benefit from cotton seed bought under the name of Lactogen. This should be got in advance.

As she gets near her time, the bitch's appetite will vary; she will feel restless and uncomfortable and not be able to settle in one place for long. Jack Russell bitches in particular are naughty about accepting the bed you have prepared for them and have very fixed ideas about what they want in this respect. If she has a favourite blanket or cushion, it may be a more peaceful solution to put it in the prepared whelping box in order to persuade her to accept it. When she does so and before she starts shredding and tearing it up, replace it with newspaper. If she won't accept this, try one of the new disposable baby nappies or the new nylon 'vet bed' which are most satisfactory for whelping on and keeps the puppies warm and dry.

Once she has finally settled to her bed, shave all the hair from her nipples, not forgetting the ones at the very top which can get caked with milk and clog up painfully. With the long-haired bitches, proper clipping of their stomachs, round the vulva and under the tail can be followed by a wash-over with warm water and a mild soap, not scented as the pups won't like sucking anything with a strong smell!

The Whelping

About twenty-four hours before her time, the bitch will go off her food, and her temperature, which is normally about 101.4°, will drop to 98° or even lower. She will whelp within a few hours now and should not be left unattended. With a sterile finger, insert a generous supply of vaseline as far inside her as possible. If you have not collected together the necessary equipment and put it all in one place, get it ready now: see later. It will be surprising what a calming effect this task will have and the knowledge that you have everything possible close to hand will be a great relief.

This is also the time to have a word with your vet. Tell him you have a Jack Russell bitch expecting her first litter and, incidentally, your first one too, and ask him if he will be available if you come up against any unusual difficulties. It is most unlikely that your bitch will need veterinary help but you may feel the need for reassurance and so ask

Fig. 6 Whelping table

Served Jan.	Whelps March	Served Feb.	Whelps April	Served March	Whelps May	Served April	Whelps June	Served May	Whelps July	Served June	Whelps Aug.	Served July	Whelps Sept.	Served Aug.	Whelps Oct.	Served Sept.	Whelps Nov.	Served Oct.	Whelps Dec.	Served Nov.	Whelps Jan.	Served Dec.	Whelps Feb.
1	5	1	5	1	3	1	3	1	3	1	3	1	2	1	3	1	3	1	3	1	3	1	2
2	6	2	6	2	4	2	4	2	4	2	4	2	3	2	4	2	4	2	4	2	4	2	3
3	7	3	7	3	5	3	5	3	5	3	5	3	4	3	5	3	5	3	5	3	5	3	4
4	8	4	8	4	6	4	6	4	6	4	6	4	5	4	6	4	6	4	6	4	6	4	5
5	9	5	9	5	7	5	7	5	7	5	7	5	6	5	7	5	7	5	7	5	7	5	6
6	10	6	10	6	8	6	8	6	8	6	8	6	7	6	8	6	8	6	8	6	8	6	7
7	11	7	11	7	9	7	9	7	9	7	9	7	8	7	9	7	9	7	9	7	9	7	8
8	12	8	12	8	10	8	10	8	10	8	10	8	9	8	10	8	10	8	10	8	10	8	9
9	13	9	13	9	11	9	11	9	11	9	11	9	10	9	11	9	11	9	11	9	11	9	10
10	14	10	14	10	12	10	12	10	12	10	12	10	11	10	12	10	12	10	12	10	12	10	11
11	15	12	15	11	13	11	13	11	13	11	13	11	12	11	13	11	13	11	13	11	13	11	12
12	16	13	16	12	14	12	14	12	14	12	14	12	13	12	14	12	14	12	14	12	14	12	13
13	17	14	17	13	15	13	15	13	15	13	15	13	14	13	15	13	15	13	15	13	15	13	14
14	18	15	18	14	16	14	16	14	16	14	16	14	15	14	16	14	16	14	16	14	16	14	15
15	19	16	19	15	17	15	17	15	17	15	17	15	16	15	17	15	17	15	17	15	17	15	16
16	20	17	20	16	18	16	18	16	18	16	18	16	17	16	18	16	18	16	18	16	18	16	17
17	21	18	21	17	19	17	19	17	19	17	19	17	18	17	19	17	19	17	19	17	19	17	18
18	22	19	22	18	20	18	20	18	20	18	20	18	19	18	20	18	20	18	20	18	20	18	19
19	23	20	23	19	21	19	21	19	21	19	21	19	20	19	21	19	21	19	21	19	21	19	20
20	24	21	24	20	22	20	22	20	22	20	22	20	21	20	22	20	22	20	22	20	22	20	21
21	25	22	25	21	23	21	23	21	23	21	23	21	22	21	23	21	23	21	23	21	23	21	22
22	26	23	26	22	24	22	24	22	24	22	24	22	23	22	24	22	24	22	24	22	24	22	23
23	27	24	27	23	25	23	25	23	25	23	25	23	24	23	25	23	25	23	25	23	25	23	24
24	28	25	28	24	26	24	26	24	26	24	26	24	25	24	26	24	26	24	26	24	26	24	25
25	29	26	29	25	27	25	27	25	27	25	27	25	26	25	27	25	27	25	27	25	27	25	26
26	30	27	30	26	28	26	28	26	28	26	28	26	27	26	28	26	28	26	28	26	28	26	27
27	31	28	1	27	29	27	29	27	29	27	29	27	28	27	29	27	29	27	29	27	29	27	28
28	1	29	2	28	30	28	30	28	30	28	30	28	29	28	30	28	30	28	30	28	30	28	1
29	2			29	31	29	1	29	31	29	31	29	30	29	31	29	1	29	31	29	31	29	2
30	3			30	1	30	2	30	1	30	1	30	1	30	1	30	2	30	1	30	1	30	3
31	4			31	2			31	2			31	2	31	2			31	2			31	4

the vet to call when the whelping is over to make sure that everything has gone back into place and there are no retained after-births or other complications.

Book the vet to dock the tails and remove the dew claws on the fifth day. Having done this, you can rest assured that your vet will give you every possible help and attention as you have done all the arranging you can possibly do at the proper time. No vet likes to be called out in the middle of the night to attend a bitch he has never heard of, who has apparently 'swallowed one of the children's balloons as there is one sticking out of her' only to find that she is in the middle of labour.

I heard of someone who called out the vet to say that her bitch was sitting in a pool of horrible black goo and wouldn't let anyone go near her. And an even more classic case of an army officer's wife who put her very pregnant bitch downstairs in the downstairs loo for the night. The next morning when she went to let the bitch out, she was so horrified to find the dog covered in blood that she shut the door in terror and screamed down the telephone for the vet. The bitch had produced four puppies and probably because she had nothing but the quarry tiles to whelp on – not even a sheet of newspaper – she had left them all in the bags and hidden herself behind the lavatory. The amazing thing is that three out of four were still alive and, once they had been taken out of the bags and the unpleasant sight of the gory afterbirths removed she came out from behind the loo and became an excellent mother.

It is with the hope that I can educate such abysmal ignorance that I give what might appear to some experienced breeders quite unnecessary details of what should be collected together.

1. A whelping box about 12in. deep, containing a hot water bottle or a little electrically-heated pad which can be bought for a few pounds and which, if wrapped around by a piece of old blanket or towelling, is an excellent way of keeping the puppies warm. Its advantages over a hot water bottle are that it is safer, keeps a steady heat for hours on end and, as it is thermostatically controlled, it cannot overheat and harm the puppies. If a hot water bottle is to be used, a kettle must be filled so that the hot water will be available. If you have a vet bed, there is no need for extra warmth. For a Jack Russell, an 18in. by 12in. is sufficient.

2. Scissors for cutting the cords and thread to tie them up.

3. Roll of cotton wool or a roll of kitchen paper towelling.

4. Packet of J-cloths – a most useful commodity for gripping the puppy as it is being born. Excellent for rubbing life into the new born puppy and soft enough for use in wiping the nose and mouth clear of fluid.

5. Bottle of hydrogen of peroxide or iodine or a styptic pencil. Useful for dabbing on the cord to stop bleeding.

6. Surgical clips in case the cord gets cut while the after-birth is still inside the bitch. The clamps will prevent the broken end of the cord disappearing back inside her.

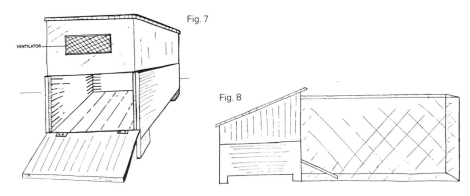

Fig. 7

VENTILATOR

Fig. 8

Fig. 7   Whelping box with infra-red lamp removed and perspex top in place

Fig. 8   Whelping box with run attached

7.   Flask of coffee or tea as the bitch should not be left while you make it.

8.   Small quantity of brandy or whisky which may be required to revive a failing pup and will be found invaluable to boost yours and the bitch's morale in the wee small hours!

9.   Book, playing cards or knitting as the waiting may be prolonged and it is essential that you keep awake.

10. Clock or watch.

11. Pail with lid or cover for taking away the afterbirths and messy bedding.

12. Plenty of fresh newspaper and a new cardboard box for when the first comes to a sticky end. A large blanket to place over the box afterwards.

The temperature of the room for whelping should be 75° to 80° and it is most important that a constant heat is maintained as a chill to the bitch or puppies is very harmful at this stage. The puppies come from a warm place and when they are wet and reach a lower temperature they can catch a chill very easily and then develop pneumonia in a matter of hours. It is better to be too hot than too cold, so have an infra-red heater overhead if possible or place the whelping box next to a boiler, radiator or electric fire.

Before settling down in the warm, take her outside to relieve herself but stay with her or she might go off to somewhere inaccessible in order to have her puppies in a quiet dark place. I once had to get two men with crowbars to lift a large concrete step under which one of my bitches was just about to establish a labour ward.

When she returns to her whelping box, she will probably start to pant but will refuse the drink of water you offer her. She will even shiver and tear into her bedding as though she has gone berserk. This is good. The harder she digs, the easier will be her labour pains. When she eventually lies down quite quietly on her side and slightly stiffens her tail, she is really about to begin. Don't take your eyes off her now. See that the electric light does not glare into her eyes but leave yourself enough light to see what is happening under her tail. With a first whelping, a puppy can protrude for some time and no one be any the wiser.

It may be as well here to explain a little about the mechanics of whelping since I hope this will prove to be an instructive book for anyone who seriously wants to breed Jack Russells and has no knowledgeable person handy except the vet. As the whelping may well be in the early hours of the morning when even your nearest and dearest are not at their most helpful, you may not know *exactly* what to expect.

What actually happens is that after a time of stiffening her tail and arching her back and bearing down, she will suddenly be seen to have a slimy black bladder sticking out between her back legs. This may stay there seemingly unnoticed for quite some time. If, on closer examination, you find that it is clear, it will be the water bladder. If you can't see through it and, when pressing it, a hard form is felt inside the bubble, this will be the first puppy. If it stays there for some minutes, it will be as well to look closer to see if it is the head end or the foot that is protruding. The head usually comes out with some force but a foot first will mean a breach-birth which can be a much slower process and you may need assistance.

The uterus is like a letter 'Y'. The two arms are called the horns and this is where the puppies wait to be born. The cervix is the point where these two horns meet and this leads into the leg of the Y or the vagina, and this in turn leads to the vulva, through which the puppy has to pass to be born. Each puppy is contained in a sac of fluid which is attached to him at the navel by a cord – known as the umbilical cord. This membrane has been the means by which nourishment has passed into the developing puppy from the mother, from the placenta which is attached to the wall of the uterus.

The pups are distributed in both horns and, when delivery commences, the cervix relaxes and spasms of muscular pressure force the first puppy in the horn right down the passage and out through the vulva. The next pup comes from the opposite horn and they continue coming from opposite sides until the whelping is completed. Sometimes two come quite quickly and then there is an indefinite interval before the next pair make their appearance, so the whole thing can be over in less than an hour or may last for several hours.

It is often very trying for the attendant to know how long to wait in case the hold-up is a serious one. For the beginner, I would suggest that two hours is long enough to require advice, two to four hours is stretching it a bit but can be from quite normal causes. A vet would much rather be called unnecessarily than not until things are so serious that the bitch has been straining for such a long time that she is exhausted and would make a doubtful subject for a forceps delivery or, worse still, a Caesarean operation.

When things are normal, as soon as the sac appears, the bitch will lick it and the minute you hear a very squelchy, watery noise you know that she has got the puppy out completely and is busy on her mopping-up operation. She will pull the sac off the puppy, bouncing him up and down quite relentlessly while she chews on the umbilical cord which eventually she breaks off near its navel. With luck, she will leave about two inches of cord and the action of her teeth will seal the ends of the cord so that they do not bleed. If she tears the cord too close to the body, it will be sure to bleed copiously and this must be stopped at once by tying some cotton round it very tightly, making a double knot. If she has torn it so much that there is not enough skin to tie, seal the hole as quickly as possible or the pup will bleed to death. Iodine or peroxide have both been found to be effective sealers. Powdered permanganate of potash or gentian violet are also remedies, the latter being slightly messy. A preparation called 'Newskin' has also proved effective.

Having seen to the cord, the bitch should be attended to next. She will probably now be eating the placenta, or after-birth. Some schools of thought think this is a good thing to let her do whilst others prefer not to let her eat them. In the days before the dog became domesticated, the bitch would eat all the placentas and these would supply her with enough nourishment to keep her alive while she was in too weak a state to hunt and catch food for herself. There is reason to believe that something in the placenta stimulates contraction of the uterus to help delivery, so let her eat the first placenta and then the others should be taken away. I like to get them out of the way quickly as they are very unpleasant looking things and very messy to handle. You should roll them up in plenty of newspaper and burn them as soon as possible.

Each puppy has a placenta and it is important that one for each birth is accounted for. If one gets left behind, or the cord breaks off, it may come with the next pup. If there is one short when all the puppies are born, the vet must be called and the bitch will be given an injection which will make her expel it. Failure to do this will cause her to be severely ill and could end in her death.

My experience with Jack Russell bitches has been that while they produce their puppies easily enough, they are so energetic with the cord and bounce the pups about so vigorously that although they get them breathing satisfactorily, they are apt to damage the navels and cause umbilical hernias or worse. One bitch shook a pup so hard in her effort to gnaw off the cord that she pulled its insides out. Not many of them would do this and hundreds of puppies are born without any such dramas happening. However, to make sure they don't, I prefer to take steps to help the mother.

Instead of letting the bitch pull the puppy out herself, I have ready a piece of old muslin napkin, or a J-cloth, and with this I catch the puppy as it is being expelled. If it is slow arriving, I take what is showing into the palm of my hand which is covered by the soft cloth, and I very gently ease out the puppy, taking great care not to break off the umbilical cord. Once the pup is out, I quickly break the skin covering its head, and with my finger wipe its mouth open. If the after-birth is still inside the bitch, I hold the pup upside down to let its lungs clear of fluid, and I hold on tight to that part of the cord that is sticking out of the vulva. If, after several minutes, nothing happens, I try to ease the afterbirth out by myself.

As soon as I have done this, I quickly wipe out the pup's mouth, clear its nostrils and rub it well with a piece of soft towelling to bring the life into it. I work on the cord, holding it firmly in my left hand with my thumb and fingers round the puppy's body and I use the nails of the thumb and first finger on my right hand to sever the cord. My vet told me this was better than cutting. Sometimes the cords are very tough so I am forced to cut them.

If the puppy has been a long time being born, or the mother isn't interested into licking life into him, which they usually do readily enough, it may be necessary to take quite strong measures to get the puppy breathing. Clear his nose and mouth, rub him vigorously with the towelling, moving towards his heart. Wrap him in the towelling, in case his wet body slips out of your hands, and hold him upside down. If no mucus drains out of him as it should, shake him well and swing him, still upside down, to dislodge the fluid. Keep wiping his nose and mouth, rub his body and swing. After a few minutes of this, if he is still not breathing, take him by the cord – holding it close to his body – and pull quite gently. After a few times, press on his chest and then on the cord and repeat for as long as necessary. Quite dead-looking puppies will respond to this treatment. It can be kept up for an hour or so depending on how clogged-up his lungs are, as you must drain them to bring him to life.

Once you feel the puppy 'bend' you know you are winning and he will soon start to breathe. If he cries, all the better as it will help him to fill his lungs with air. Once breathing has been established, give the pup to the bitch so that she can lick him and get his organs working. However dead he looked a moment ago, he will soon be struggling to find the teat and will be sucking away in no time.

Let the newly born pups stay with the mother while waiting for whelping to continue but, as soon as she starts to produce another puppy, take the first ones away and put them on the warm pad or near the electric heater or hot water bottle wrapped in a piece of blanket. Make a sort of envelope so that they can be popped inside and covered up to keep warm – it will also keep them quiet so as not to upset the mother who will have enough to be getting on with. Clear all the mess away and don't let the bitch have back the first pups until she is clean. While she nuzzles them and tries to get them to feed, check on the last born and get it dried off and breathing properly before putting it down with its mother. And don't forget to keep a count on those afterbirths!

When you think the bitch has finished whelping, feel her for any hard-lumps the same shape as one of the puppies you held in the palm of your hand. If quite soft, it is safe to leave her. If, however, there is still a hardness inside her and she still looks unsettled, give her an hour or two to get going herself and then, if nothing happens, summon your vet. If the trouble is that one of the puppies is stuck at the top of the cervix, he may be able to produce it with forceps. Sometimes two puppies try to get down the tunnel together and get wedged. A clever vet can push one back and allow the first to descend. If there is a dead pup, it is more dangerous and the health of the mother and the other pups can be seriously affected. Toy breeds and bull-headed ones are prone to this kind of trouble because of the size of their heads, but Jack Russells have narrow heads which make for easy whelping. Very fat bitches and ones that have had a very protracted labour often suffer from inertia but this is very rare in terriers who are so active. Injections of pitruitin will stimulate the muscles and should help to get things moving, but your vet will tell you if this is necessary.

If your vet recommends a Caesarean, he will have explored all the other avenues and, if you are sensible, you will agree at once as the decision will be yours. Any delay will add to the danger and the sooner the operation is performed the better will be the chances for the bitch and also for getting live puppies. Nobody can pretend that this is not a very serious and often dangerous operation but thousands are performed successfully and the speed with which your bitch will recover will amaze you. The puppies, not having to struggle, will be all right too but must be kept away from the effects of the anaesthetic.

Post Whelping Period

New born puppies that have been born normally are usually quiet and very contented. A small to medium litter will have plenty of room to have a teat each and soon only the sound of sucking will be heard. If a pup keeps on crying, there will probably be something wrong with it – he may be small and keep being pushed off his teat by the bigger, stronger pups. Hold him on a few times and give him time to get a good feed. This is especially important in the beginning as the first milk, or colostrum, contains all the antibodies the mother has built up in her own system and which gives the pup immunity to distemper and hardpad as they absorb her immunities with her milk.

Before leaving her to settle down, the bitch should be taken outside to relieve herself and the bed can then be put to rights. If the cardboard box is very soiled, it can be replaced and new bedding inserted.

It is hoped that she will be an excellent mother and her pups will thrive and give no trouble. The chances are that she will and, once you start a regular routine to feed her every four hours and to let her out at frequent and regular intervals, the pups will make surprising progress.

People who mate a bitch for their own benefit must always bear in mind that they owe her every consideration and help through all the time she is carrying and during and after whelping. You should make a careful examination of her condition the next day to ensure that she has no temperature and that her milk is flowing freely from unclogged teats. This will guard her against any inflammation of the womb or metritis, pymetria, mastitis or inflammation of the milk glands. Her teats must be sponged with clean, warm water daily and her hindquarters and tail sponged at the same time with a very mild solution of Cetavlon. She will more readily settle down to the next job of rearing her new litter happily if she feels clean and comfortable and can trust you to attend to her needs. You should also keep outsiders away from her precious family so that she doesn't need to upset herself defending them, as she will be only too ready to do.

When the mother has rested from her labours and shows interest in eating and drinking again, offer her some warm milk and glucose with Bengers Food, Complan, or Farex with Complan mixed in. Make sure she has clean water to drink at all times. You will have to feed her in her box as she will not leave her pups to eat or drink. She must leave them to go outside though and this part of her management is most important. She will be eating and drinking more so will want to go outside regularly. Every two hours is not too often in the first few days, especially first thing in the morning and last thing at night as a normally house-clean bitch will worry if she is forced to mess indoors.

Every feed should have a pinch of SA 37 and she should have olive oil or fish oil to keep her insides lubricated as the lack of exercise may make her constipated.

When she is outside is the best time to examine the pups to make sure they are not malformed in any way. A crying pup who has enough food available may have a cleft palate. Open his mouth wide and with a good light shining in, see if there is a triangular hole at the back of the roof of his mouth. Hare lip and cleft palate go together and stop the puppy sucking. You should ask the vet to look at the puppy and unless the puppy is valuable as a prospective worker, it is usually kindest to put him down. However, if it is decided to try to keep him, he can be fed with a tube on the end of a hypodermic syringe. The vet will show you what to do. Measure the tube from his mouth to his navel and push the end of the tube down the back of his throat waiting for him to swallow to get it down. Take plenty of time and make up a syringe full of Lactol or another milk substitute and slowly let the mixture through by pressing the plunger. A clear tube made of polystyrene is better than a rubber one as bubbles can be seen and cleared. The tube and syringe must be *full*. Fill the stomach till it is very firm. Withdraw the tube and wash out immediately and soak all in a Milton solution or sterilise.

This method of feeding can be used on orphaned pups and, once the operation has been successfully accomplished a few times, it will be found to be the most effective way of feeding very young pups as there is no danger of the milk going down the wrong way, blocking the windpipe and so cutting off the puppy's air supply. Many puppies die when supplementary feeding has to be practised as the liquid gets to the lungs and the result is pneumonia.

If there is no cleft palate but a puppy still cries, this will upset the mother and, unless the squeaker is given attention without delay, she may start picking him up in her mouth in order to quieten him. If she is rough, her teeth could damage him and, while he is in her mouth, he can't get any nourishment and so will soon fade. People say a bitch always knows if there is something wrong with a puppy and picks it out to die. I have known bitches accept a squeaker without hesitation once it has been pacified and filled up with food, so it needn't always mean the end of one of the pups.

Her milk may take a few days to come steadily, but soon the pups will all receive their fair share and the more they suck the more milk she will produce. On the other hand, if they do not take milk readily, it will dry up and disappear very quickly. Reluctant puppies and squeakers are best held on the teats every few hours to make sure they do feed.

A greenish vaginal discharge from the bitch is nothing to be alarmed about and she will also lose blood for some time. A discharge which seems too plentiful is a danger sign and should be reported to the vet.

Keep the bitch in her whelping box. A blanket over the top will give her a feeling of privacy, which is very important. Keep other dogs, animals and strangers well away. While the puppy proudness lasts, she is quite capable of killing another bitch's puppies out of jealousy, however mild a nature she has at normal times. If anyone she does not know or trust touches her precious babies, she will quite likely snap. Puppy pride is a natural sentiment for a new mother and it must be allowed for up to a point, but biting might lead to a permanent bad habit and an innocent child might get seriously hurt from a really bad bite. Outsiders, and even members of her own family, must be introduced carefully and gradually. If one of the children is allowed to hold a puppy while you are with her, she will grow accustomed to the idea and it is better for several people to look after her rather than just one.

Careful watch should be kept to check that she shows no sign of eclampsia. This is an imbalance in the calcium content in the blood which shows itself at the start with very rapid breathing, restlessness, trembling, crying and her eyes will take on a 'glassy' look. If not halted by veterinary attention at this stage, when a single injection of calcium gluconate into the muscle will act like magic, she will deteriorate quickly and start to stagger and stiffen in her legs. Soon she will be in convulsions and death is very near. Even if she seems to recover completely, she can still start again. I had a Yorkshire Terrier bitch who had been injected and recovered but died in the night because we left her within sight of her pups instead of taking her completely away. She became upset which brought on another attack. I have never had any trouble with a Jack Russell because they are never fussy with their food like the Yorkies and their history doesn't record that in years gone by, in order to make them small, they were kept short of the necessary supplements which might have made them big and strong.

In a book such as this, the aim is not to frighten but to explain all the possible contingencies so that, should the worst happen, it could be recognised in time to save a life.

Breeders of Jack Russells are lucky, for their job is seldom very troublesome. Given plenty of food, the bitch will make plenty of milk. If she only has one or two puppies and something isn't done to restrict the supply, she will become engorged and her breasts will become acutely painful. Her diet and liquid intake must be drastically cut down. I find honey water – a teaspoonful of honey in two tablespoons of warm water – given in sips at intervals through the day better than outright starving. It is being cruel to be kind, for everything she eats and drinks will go straight to the milk glands. As there are not enough puppies to draw off sufficient milk to ease the situation, the only thing to do is to lessen stimulation. Warm olive oil can be massaged into the glands and this will relieve the tautness. The temptation to milk out the teats to ease them should be avoided as it will only cause more milk to be made. Serious congestion, with a rise in temperature, may need antibiotics to put it right.

An infra-red lamp should be kept over the whelping box all the time for a month if in winter and then less in the day and only at night until they are eight weeks old. In summer, the first two weeks should be under constant heat but the lamp can be raised higher and higher. The light from the lamp helps the bitch at night as she can see if a puppy moves away and is able to avoid stepping on them. She may not like the heat much but it is essential to keep the puppies constantly warm. If she gets too uncomfortable, she can be given another box to sleep in slightly away from the heat but near enough to be able to keep a watchful eye on her charges.

Her duties will be to keep the puppies clean – licking them will do this – and also encourage them to pass their motions and urine. She will keep her own bed clean while she alone is feeding the pups. When weaning starts, she will leave you to clear up after the feeding but she will still lick her puppies clean.

If a mother seems anxious to get rid of her litter before they are five to six weeks old, it is either because she doesn't feel strong enough to look after them any more or, most likely, because nobody has thought to cut the puppies' nails which scratch the poor mother underneath and so cause her to dry up the milk bar. Cutting the nails at regular intervals is important too where children's bare legs and ladies stockings are concerned. If this is always done regularly, the pups won't mind and all who come in contact with them will be much happier and more comfortable. Imagine how alarming it is for a very young puppy who puts his paws on people in order to show his trust and affection only to have them screech in pain and push him off. He won't know his claws are sharp as little needles. It is up to his owner to see they are kept short. A pair of tiny curved nail scissors is right for very young nails and a nail cutter, like the one illustrated, will be necessary when the nails reach the hardness of adulthood. Plenty of road walking will keep the nails under control but if the dog is exercised only on grass, they will need extra attention.

Weaning

The first sign that weaning is near will be when the bitch regurgitates her food for the puppies. This isn't as horrible as it sounds, for Nature has seen that the first solid food the puppies get has been predigested for them. The mother must be fed finely minced meat and a few brown breadcrumbs. When she brings it up, this will be just the right consistency and the temperature for the pups and they will set about eating it with relish. Make sure that the bitch is taken right away from her litter for an hour or two at this stage and given enough nourishment for her own needs.

As the puppies take more food, the mother won't need to make so much milk. Care should be taken that she doesn't get used to eating the large quantities of food as she will get fat and lazy. Regularise the feeding – giving more raw meat and much less biscuit; then reduce the meat until she is getting what she eats normally. Her exercise must be increased daily until she is back in her usual fit form and her stomach and teats go back in place and not hanging down. You have then done your best for her.

Docking

At about the fifth day, it is advisable to have the puppies' tails docked and to remove the dew claws. An inexperienced breeder should ask the vet to perform this simple operation and no one should attempt it unless they have had extensive veterinary supervision. At the moment, the Veterinary Association is still allowing tails to be docked but measures are afoot to ban the practice. Long tails detract quite a lot from the smartness of this little terrier and a shortened tail, but not too short, gives an excellent means of pulling him out of fox and rabbit holes.

Tails are shortened about one-third but it is necessary to judge each pup as an individual and make the cut at the best place to suit the particular puppy. Hold the puppy up by the head and tail and see what looks best. Mark the spot with a felt pen or tie some cotton round the spot so that the vet can cut in the proper place. If you do the operation yourself, you will need a pair of docking scissors for the tails and a small pair of curved scissors for the dew claws. The scissors should be thoroughly sterilised by boiling in a saucepan of water for about ten minutes. Leave to cool and then dry thoroughly if using ground permanganate of potash as a sealer as this makes a terrible mess when wet. I use a styptic pencil and rub it over the cut places and this stops bleeding and seals the whole thing up neatly. The mother should be removed well away before this operation commences. The pups won't feel any pain as the bones are only gristle at this stage, but left until older, it entails a severe operation. This might prove a shock to the dog's system and needs stitches to close up the cut places. Although we are not dealing with show dogs, the docked tails enhance the terriers' appearance and give a much smarter outline.

Dew claws are extra thumbs which, when the dog was in its evolution, were probably used for climbing. Today they are nothing but a nuisance as they catch in brambles and get the dog caught up in all sorts of difficulties. The dew claws should be removed, joint and all, or they will grow again. Cut under the little cushion that holds the claw and remove it completely. Seal with the styptic pencil or permanganate of potash. It is essential that the latter is finely ground otherwise the coarse grains will fall off, the blood will seep through and it will not seal completely. The aim is to have no loss of blood at all.

Parson Jack Russell required his terriers to have tails that would fit the huntsman's hand so that he could easily pull then out of holes. The people who hunt their terriers and enter them underground often do not have the dew claws removed as they maintain that they help the dog to climb the steep drops which are part of the strategic defence of the fox's stronghold. If a hunt terrier is deprived of his front dew claws, it is felt that he could have difficulty in climbing out of these drops and, unless found and dug out, he could die a miserable death.

The Fell and Moorland Working Terrier Club was formed with the express intention of supplying the means of rescuing trapped terriers. An excellent idea which could be copied by interested bodies in other parts of the country where this kind of tragedy can happen.

8 Care and Management of the New Born Puppy

If the bitch is well-nourished and has a reasonably small litter, the pups won't need any extra feeding until they are five weeks old as she will be able to supply all their needs. Some breeders like to get the weaning started at three weeks and offer scraped meat or milky foods. If the bitch is feeding them properly, they won't be interested in the extras offered. If the bitch continues to be fed in her bed, the day will come when the pups will put their heads in her dish and start helping themselves.

This is the time to start weaning seriously, starting with raw scraped meat at the 2 p.m. feed which is a good one to begin with as the bitch can be taken away for a few hours. Next give a milky formula for breakfast and continue for a few days and then give another milky feed in the evening and end the weaning period with a fourth feed giving meat this time. As soon as the mother's milk starts to dry up, the puppies should be left with a milky feed for the night.

At birth, the pups will have their eyes shut and their ears closed. After nine or ten days, the eyes begin to open but the hearing doesn't come until the twenty-first day. Eyes should be watched for any stickiness which should be bathed in warm water. In-growing eyelashes can cause the eyes to water and become irritated. You can usually pluck these eyelashes out.

When they are about four weeks old, the puppies will begin to stand up and stagger about, so the box should be checked in case they fall out. They will have doubled their birth weight, their coats should be glossy with definate signs of wire or smooths emerging. The markings are now clear and the nose and eye rims and lips should be well pigmented.

Worming
The puppies should be wormed at about this time – when they are four weeks old. All puppies would appear to be born with round worms. The bonniest and huskiest ones nearly always have the most. Don't think that because they look well and you have seen no sign of worms and they never drag their bottoms along the ground they don't have worms. They are almost bound to, however carefully you have dosed

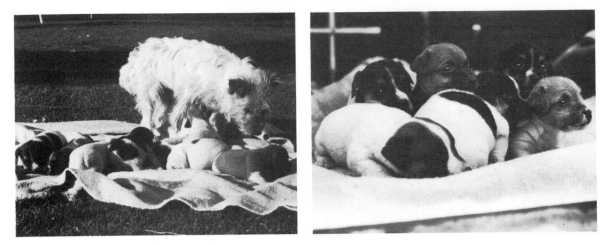

Right: A lovely litter of Jack Russell puppies bred by Mrs Horner.

Left: Pit checking up on her brood. She is not sure that they are old enough to be outside to be photographed. Pit is a splendid example of a true rough-coated Jack Russell.

the mother. If wormed at three to four weeks old with Coopane, or one of the 'safe' vermifuges, it will discourage the worms and, if a second dose is given seven to eight days later, they will be reduced – I cannot promise complete elimination as the worm eggs may get on the coat and be licked up and the whole vicious circle set in motion again. There is no point in waiting to dose the puppy until he has a glaring coat, running eyes, worm cough and is generally out of sorts by being infested with worms, as this dangerous condition can be avoided. Healthy puppies throw off the effect of worming as soon as the drug goes through the bloodstream.

The dose is given *after* feeding. Give one tablet for 10lb. of bodyweight. The pup at this stage will require about a quarter of a tablet. I crush it up into milk and let it trickle down the side of the mouth, making a pouch with the lips. If another drink is given straight away it helps it down and avoids him bringing up the dose. Pushing the bit of pill down can do a lot of damage to his little throat and will often be brought up again. The mother is best kept away from the puppies at this time and their beds and runs should be covered in newspaper only. Everything they pass should be examined for worms and then burned immediately. Have plenty of clean paper ready as it will probably take several days before they pass all the worms they have. It is *most important* that this treatment is repeated the following week and this time the dose should be increased very slightly.

Teeth

About this time they begin to get their teeth. They should be given large marrow bones to chew on, just as babies enjoy teething rings. They usually cut their teeth quite painlessly but if they seem to be in trouble with their teeth not coming through quickly and their gums are red and sore, a daily dose of bone meal or lime water and cod liver oil will be of great help. Teething goes on for several weeks and if they get a rash or seem to run a temperature, a regular twice-weekly dose of magnesia will act as a cooling agent.

On the subject of teething, it is important to check the teeth and make sure that the bite is correct so you can inform prospective owners. This means that the terrier mouth should have a scissor bite – the top teeth fitting closely over the bottom ones. If they are level it is not a bad fault but if the bottom teeth are over the top ones, this is called under-shot and is a bad fault in a terrier as it stops them holding on to things properly.

Ears fly in all directions while teeth are being cut so it is best not to be too critical of any poor ear carriage until all the teeth are through. The Jack Russell should carry his ears tipped over but he may stick them up straight for a while until his milk teeth have all come through.

All puppies should be given plenty of space and opportunity for play – this is as important a part of their development as resting and sleeping. After a vigorous playtime, the pups will need to rest completely and renew their energy for the next time. Children should be told not to interfere with this rest period or the puppy could grow up quite neurotic and the rest is necessary for it to achieve 'condition'. This can be checked by running the fingers down the inside of the foreleg. If a growing puppy is 'running off' its food, the blade of the bone will be sharp. If his condition is adequate, there will be a pad of flesh all along the blade and this is the sign that he is in good condition. This is a good tip to remember when you are buying a puppy.

Early house training should now start and full details of this will be found in Chapter Six – Training the Jack Russell Terrier.

A bitch will teach her family to play.

Ridley Redwing at
ten weeks. Bred by
Mrs S. M. Atter.

Inoculations

It will be now that you should arrange for the puppies to be inoculated
against parvo virus, hard pad, distemper, hepatitis and leptospiral
jaundice. Luckily these are all combined in one injection, followed by
a second part of the lepto done about two weeks later. The puppies
should be done when they are ten to twelve weeks old; it can be done
sooner but there is no guarantee that it won't be ineffective if the pup
is still feeding off his mother and still receiving her natural immunity
through her milk.

Inoculations have to be given by the vet. Anyone who has had the
horrible experience of nursing cases of these terrible infections before
the days of safe vaccines will agree that, however much it costs, all
puppies must be given this protection as a birthright.

If you are selling your puppies, give the new owners the inoculation
certificate. If a puppy is sold before being inoculated, the new owner
must be warned not to take the puppy outside the confines of the house
or where other dogs have been, until he has been given the necessary
injections. More information about inoculations will be found on page
76.

9 Finding Homes for the Puppies

At the end of the second month is the time that most puppies go to new homes, and if you have decided to sell some of your bitch's litter, you should have already made arrangements. If you are keeping one – or more – for yourself, it will be difficult to decide which one if it is your first litter. A knowledgeable breeder or the owner of the stud dog will, no doubt, enjoy helping you in this respect. Don't keep the smallest because he is the sweetest as he may not be as sturdy as one of the larger ones. Pick one that is lightly marked and of a happy, extrovert disposition. Make sure his body is round and firm when you pick him up; don't choose a yapper or a scrapper. All the different traits of character will be obvious by the time they are seven or eight weeks old and they will be chronic little time-wasters but lots of fun to watch.

Of course, you may have friends who have already asked to be kept a puppy from your litter and having chosen any you want to keep, let them have second choice. But just because they are friends, you should not let them have the puppy until it is at least eight weeks old.

Puppies are at their most appealing stage between eight and twelve weeks old and, as long as you get people who are really interested in buying a puppy of the type you have to offer, there should be no difficulty in selling them quickly. In fact, it will surprise you just how soon good puppies can be sold.

I once had a litter of four and sold one to the owner of our country garage. He had a field beside his property and his little daughter was playing with her new puppy there when one of the garage customers asked if there were any more for sale as it was just the sort of pup he had been looking for. I soon satisfied myself that he had the right sort of home for a puppy and he went off with another dog pup, leaving me with two bitches which I was quite happy to run on for my own breeding. That evening, the garage owner's married son came to see if we still had another dog puppy and he departed with one of the bitches and the next morning a neighbouring farmer saw the one at the garage and came along to claim my last remaining puppy. All these people lived in the neighbourhood except the customer at the garage who lived

Left: 'Let's play tug-o-war'. The author's grandson with Gilly who loves this game.

Right: A cardboard box full of mischief.

in another part of the country but who always made a point of stopping at the garage when passing through to compare notes, and we have had friendly relations with all the owners ever since. This was an example of good, happy out-going little puppies who had been well-reared and had every care and attention, becoming their own publicity agents. This is the best way of all.

Keep away from Puppy Dealers

Choosing the best buyers for your precious pups is one of the most important decisions you will be called upon to make when breeding for sale. Never forget that you caused these puppies to be born for your own satisfaction and you owe them the best start and the best life you can obtain for them. Parcelling them up litter by litter and flogging them off to the nearest puppy farm just isn't on. They *may* look after them all right and they *may not*. They *may* find the right sort of customers and they *may not*. The main thing is to remember that *you* will never know.

If you have a conscience at all, you will want to know what happens to your pups. With other breeds registered at the Kennel Club, it is always possible to trace registered stock, but you will never hear again how the Jack Russell pups you bred turned out. You may have done a bad job and be glad never to hear more about them, but it is just as likely that you have turned out some splendid youngsters. Then, the re-seller will take all the credit and the extra money your efforts will have entitled him to, and you will never have the satisfaction of hearing people praise your cleverness and the good job you have done. You won't have the opportunity to judge if the two parents were compatible or not and if you would have got better temperaments if you used 'A' instead of 'B' as a sire, and if that little one's ears went right after teething.

My advice, for what it is worth, is to breed as good pups as you possibly can – remembering that the difference between a good bitch and an indifferent one may be about £10 in value and the difference between the best dog and the worst may be £5 or less. For the sake of £15, you can breed good pups capable of being sold anywhere instead of breeding such rubbish that you are ashamed to meet your future buyers and so have to bundle them off to a dealer. The £15 will only be a fraction of what the dealer will be taking on your litter, so you may as well take a bit more trouble yourself and learn a few tips on how to go about selling the pups yourself, and a new dimension will be opened to you.

Advertising

It will be seen how easy it is to sell really good pups and the contents of this book are aimed at helping you to produce and rear the right kind. Advertising can be expensive but you need not aim at the readers of the most expensive magazines and dailies until you have exhausted the local papers where most people look first of all and only search the more expensive ones when they can't find what they want.

Your local pet shop will put a card in the window or on a 'For Sale' notice board. Another good place is in the newsagent's window where you will find ads for domestics, gardeners, outgrown prams and bikes, livestock of all kinds, clothes and every sort of miscellaneous back-room industry that one could imagine. This is always the first place that litters of dogs and kittens, fish and birds will be offered, apart from notices which appear in front gardens announcing 'Puppies for Sale' or 'Terrier Pups for Sale'. If you put 'Jack Russell Terriers for Sale', you may run the risk of some adherents of the original type calling in and telling you you have no such thing. But, so wide is the popularity of these little dogs, that most people reading a notice like that will have a very clear idea in their minds of what it is you are offering.

Always bear in mind that you must give a true, honest description of what you have to offer otherwise you are liable to prosecution under the Trade Description Act.

You must try to encourage buyers to come to see for themselves what good pups you have. An advertisement may be all that is necessary if the demand is as keen as is usual for Jack Russell puppies. Word the advertisement something like this:

JACK RUSSELL TERRIERS

Healthy, well-reared puppies from a good typical strain looking for kind, suitable homes. Sensible prices. Apply owner/breeder (your name, address and telephone number).

This will inform readers that you bred the pups yourself and did not buy them in for re-sale and that you have taken trouble to produce healthy stock which you have fed correctly and wormed and managed in the proper way. By mentioning 'suitable homes', you can refuse to sell to an upstairs flat or town dwelling without any garden if you feel your puppy should only live in the country or open areas where he has plenty of opportunity for out-of-door pursuits and the kind of life he was bred for. You have left a loop-hole to be able to turn down a buyer who would keep the dog in a drawing-room and only take it out when they went out to play bridge or to the local. Explain that a tiny toy breed like a Chihuahua or Peke is more suitable for this kind of life. Here, I must add, that there are Pekes and Chihuahuas of my acquaintance who would shudder at the thought of such an existence for themselves!

Selling the Puppy as a Worker

If you have seriously bred this litter to sell to people who will want to use the terrier for hunting, then a lot more work will have to go into the dog's background and all this information must somehow be included on the 'pedigree'. While it may not be essential for a 'pedigree' to be given with a Jack Russell being sold as a pet, I think it is important that one as comprehensive as possible is produced when the puppy is being purchased for working. Whilst names of breeders are not necessarily important, the achievement in the hunting and working field of the antecedents can be of considerable use. Hereditary characteristics, such as temperament, steadiness, keenness, scent and the general intelligence that is so important in the make-up of a working terrier, can all be read in a dog's background.

When you have 'working' puppies to sell with these specific characteristics, you should advertise in the specialist media such as *Shooting, Horse and Hound*, *The Field* and *Country Life*. They will, of course, command higher prices than terriers for pets.

It is a good idea to let your local hunt know that you have 'working' puppies for sale in case they know of enthusiasts looking for some young stock.

Prices of £200-300 are asked and received for good trained working terriers and the demand for them isn't confined to this country since there is an *eager* interest in them all over the world.

Selling Abroad

Often people from abroad contact you about your puppies. Those people interested in British canine activities, study reports in the relevant press. They watch specifically for blood-lines they think will match their own dogs or one they need to vary their stock.

If you get such a request, answer it promptly as such interest can quickly wane. Give an honest description of what you have to sell. If there is a fault, describe it. If you don't tell about a fault of great significance, and if your customer wastes his money buying a dog with such a fault, he would be very unlikely to do business with you again. On the other hand, he may not worry about the fault and feel that by your pointing it out, he can trust you to sell a dog with everything else right. When your clients are too far away – abroad or the other end of this country – to come to inspect the puppies, mutual trust is all important for the sake of future business. No dog is perfect and your customer knows this quite well.

The following is a Pedigree of Pandora a broken-coated tan and white bitch Jack Russell owned by Mrs Julie Edwards of Tildara, Lara, Victoria, Australia. The sire, Peter Piper was imported from the United Kingdom and was not supplied with a pedigree. In the light of the information Mrs Edwards supplies for the female side of her pedigree it will be seen how very disappointing it would be for such very dedicated breeders as Mrs Edwards to have a whole line of pedigree completely unknown. No stock should be exported without at

Fig. 9   Pedigree of Pandora

	Parents	Grandparents	Great grandparents	Great-great-grandparents	Great-great-great-grandparents
PANDORA	Sire Peter Piper (Imported from UK by Peter Dennis) 11½'' 11 lb	Sire Graysan Jack 13'' Rough-coat tan/white	Sire* Johnnie 500 Rough-coat tan/white	Sire Squeak (imported from UK by Adams)	
				Dam Bubbles (imported from UK by Adams)	
			Dam** Jill 501 Smooth-coat tan/white	Sire Unnamed dog (imported from UK by Becketts)	
				Dam Unnamed bitch (imported from UK by Becketts)	
		Dam Unknown			
	Dam Jezebel	Sire Unknown			
		Dam Mandy 11'' 14 lb Roughcoat tan/white	Sire John Henry Rough-coat tan/white	Sire Shandy (Imported from UK by Roycroft)	
				Dam Josephine	Sire * Johnnie 500 Dam** Jill 501
			Dam Greaves Midge Smooth-coat tan/white	Sire Shandy (Imported from UK by Roycroft)	
				Dam Josephine	Sire * Johnnie 500 Dam** Jill 501

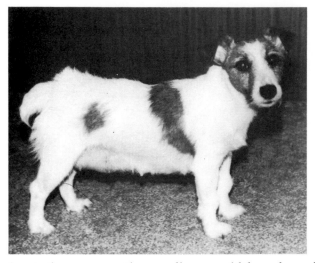

Pandora, a tan and white broken coat, heavily in whelp. Owned and bred by Julie Edwards.

least three-generation pedigrees. Although pedigrees are not usually supplied in this country, if buyers insist on them breeders will supply them. It is as simple as that.

When handling dogs going abroad, contact the Ministry of Agriculture – Export Department – at Tollworth House, Surbiton, Surrey and they will tell you if the specific country to which you are sending the puppy, has any special requirements, such as all the forms in triplicate (Germany), sworn statement that you bred the dog (South Africa) and a blood test for leptospirosis (Sweden), etc.

Regulations concerning Common Market countries are changing all the time and rather than give details here which may be out of date in six months time, it is wiser for you to contact the Ministry for all the up-to-date information.

You will need a certificate from your vet a few days before the dog is due to travel saying that it is in good health and fit. This will cost about £5 according to your vet's charges.

A box made especially for air travel will cost £10 – £20 for a full-grown Jack Russell. Food will have to be supplied for the journey with a written instruction sheet about feeding. The flight must be booked with the Cargo Booking Department of the airline being used and you must notify them several days before take-off with details of when and how the dog is to be met. Get them to give you a flight number and an Airway Bill number; notify the consignée in good time for the dog to be met and send a cable confirming that the dog is on its way. The dog should arrive at the airport several hours before take-off and the Cargo Booking Department will give you full instructions about this.

Keep the Airway Bill and Cargo receipt in case there is any query. If

Two Swedish Skäne Terriers – an unrecognised breed that has been in existance since the 18th century. They are farm dogs, brilliant ratters and go to ground readily. A club of 300 keeps the breed up to a high standard. They are content not to be accepted by the Swedish Kennel Club in case they lost their working ability.

you prefer not to do the arranging yourself, there are excellent firms to take matters completely off your hands – but their charges are high. The R.S.P.C.A. has a very good centre at Heathrow, London, in case dogs miss their planes and have to stay for some time before new arrangements are made.

Anyone who puts their mind to it, can have a very enjoyable hobby, make a lot of contacts in other countries and end up by being something of an authority on a breed that is so remarkable as to be one of the most popular in the country, even though it is outside the jurisdiction of the Kennel Club and has no definite blueprint.

It is your responsibility to see that the puppies are sold to people who are conscious of the exacting task they are undertaking in buying the baby terrier. Be sure to give every buyer a feeding chart and the times he is used to being fed and exercised. Tell them how you have started to house-train him (see page 90) so they can continue on the same lines. Warn them about leaving door and gates open and impress the importance of letting the puppy have a lot of rest and not allowing children to handle him roughly and frighten him. Care must always be taken not to push the puppy's limbs out of shape while holding him; never pull him by a leg or pick him up by the scruff of the neck.

Many people will not have heard much about Parson Jack Russell and just accept the 'Jack Russell Terrier' as a type of small game terrier that they constantly see about. They don't just buy because they think the dog is descended from the famous parson's original strain but rather because they admire it for its many obvious qualities and endearing ways. The Jack Russell today has built up its own reputation all by itself and has gained its present popularity purely on its own merits.

The approved method of presenting a pedigree is illustrated overleaf on the registration form. Pedigree forms can be obtained from pet shops who usually give them away to advertise pet foods. A pedigree is officially a record of a *pure-bred* dog's ancestry; since the Jack Russell Terrier is not yet considered 'pure-bred', these pedigrees should really be referred to as breeding charts or genealogical tables.

Parson Jack Russell Terrier Club

TERRIER REGISTRATION: Fee £1.00 per terrier | *Address of B.R.O:* Mrs. S.M. After

Details of Owner *BLOCK CAPITALS* — *If ownership changes, send this form to the B.R.O. with £1.00. and new details.*

NAME ______________ *Phone no.* ______

ADDRESS ______________ *Postcode* ______

Name of terrier being registered *No more than 24 letters*	Sex	Colour

SIGNATURE of Owner *who guarantees the information given to be correct:* ______	Date of mating	Date of birth

DETAILS OF BREEDER *(if different from above)* — *Phone no.* ______

NAME ______________

ADDRESS ______________ *Postcode* ______

Confirmation of Mating:	For official use only
SIGNATURE of Owner of Sire: ______	
If unobtainable, please state reason.	Registration number:

Parents	*Grandparents*	*Great Grandparents*
Name of Sire: Reg. No. Name and address of Owner:	Sire	Sire
		Dam
	Dam	Sire
		Dam
Name of Dam Reg. No. Name and address of Owner:	Sire	Sire
		Dam
	Dam	Sire
		Dam

Fig. 10 Parson Jack Russell Terrier Club registration form.

Besides giving new owners a pedigree, you should also give them a certificate of inoculation, along with instructions for the boosters needed.

The Jack Russell Terrier as a breed has still not found favour with the Kennel Club although they are increasingly popular with the dog buying public. It has even been the choice of the Prince and Princess of Wales. Their Jack Russell, Tiggar, obtained in 1986, is the much-loved companion of the young Princes.

Sir Geoffrey and Lady Howe had a Jack Russell Terrier, Quinton Dog, which they bought for their daughter to make up for the fact that they had to leave her alone a lot during election time. He lived to be fourteen. Then the daughter's fiancé gave them Budget when Sir Geoffrey was Chancellor of the Exchequer. Budget sired some very good-looking puppies. After his death, Sir Geoffrey and Lady Howe were given another Jack Russell puppy, grand-sired by Budget, which they have appropriately named Summit now that Sir Geoffrey is Foreign Secretary.

Another important Jack Russell Terrier is Bendicks. He was chosen by the Duke of York as a companion for the Duchess when she was expecting her first baby.

Sir Geoffrey Howe with Budget standing on the Budget Box.

10 Illnesses and Accidents

Jack Russells are normally a very strong healthy lot of dogs and the following list of ailments is more to assist in deciding what he hasn't got rather than what he has!

It is easy to see if all is not right with a sick dog as his eyes will be dull, his coat will stand up in an odd way (stare, we call it), his tail will hang down and his shoulders will hump up. There will be no bounce in his walk and the lead or his ball will hold no interest for him. Neither will food. The first thing is to take his temperature and put him in a quiet room where he won't be worried by children or other animals. Put him somewhere warm and when he has to go outside, go with him. Examine anything he passes for reference to your vet and get him back inside as quickly as possible.

If his temperature is above or below 101.4° or if he is vomiting or scouring, the sooner you get veterinary advice, the better. Don't offer him food until he goes looking for it. A rest won't do his stomach any harm.

If the vet thinks he has an infectious illness, such as kennel cough or tonsillitis or any other illness that might be catching, keep him isolated and let just one person look after him. This way, any change in his condition will be noticed immediately.

Keep his dish and water bowl apart and wash them immediately after use with Milton in the water. Give him a disposable bed and old jerseys to lie on that can be burnt later. Check his temperature twice daily and write it down: count out his day's allowance of pills into a separate bottle so you don't over-or under-dose. If the vet puts him on antibiotics, remember that there will be no lasting cure unless he takes them all for at least five days. If he seems better after two days, don't stop the pills but continue until the end of the course.

A dog hates to be ill, so give him plenty of sympathy and stroke his head gently – sick dogs seem to get some comfort from this. Feed him according to the vet's instructions. Give a plain light diet for several days after his appetite returns and stop all oils and fat if he is at all gastric.

Pills can be put under the tongue, his head held back and his throat stroked. Give liquid medicines by making a pouch with his lip and pouring the medcine in gradually, waiting for the swallow before letting any more go down. There is an excellent spoon on the market with a little tube at the end for giving medicines. Some medicines are so messy that the dog needs wrapping in a towel before dosing.

If it is necessary to stop him scratching, tie his feet up in several thicknesses of old stockings. They can make covers for the plasters on broken bones, too.

Abrasions and Cuts
Clean with a sterile swab in a fifty-fifty solution of water and Hydrogen of Peroxide, or a mild disinfectant. Cover with gauze or a mild healing ointment – such as Savlon.

Accidents
Treat for shock (qv). Keep the dog perfectly still in case of broken bones and send for the vet. More damage is done by moving him than in keeping him still and unless a dog is bleeding to death, he is best covered over to keep warm.

Acidosis
A magnesium deficiency can cause this and if charcoal is added to the diet, the condition should improve at once.

Adder Bites
The adder is the only dangerous snake in this country. Its bite should be treated without delay. Permanganate of potash pressed on the bite will hold up things until assistance is at hand. If the vet is too far away, the nearest doctor or hospital should be alerted for serum to be ready as soon as possible. Delay can cause death from severe haemorrhage or fluid on the lungs (oedema). It is important to delay the passage of the venom towards the heart. A tourniquet above the fang marks is one way, or another is cutting crosses in the swelling and squeezing the blood and venom out as quickly as possible. It is better to get to the nearest medical help as soon as you can, for timely specialised help can work wonders.

Anaemia
This is a lack of red corpuscles in the blood; an iron deficiency. Give Parrish's Food or Benbows. Liver given daily will prevent this condition but can cause scouring if fed raw.

Anal Glands, Swollen
Caused by the accumulation of secretion. If they can be squeezed out, the condition improves. Bathe them with warm water before attempting to empty them, or take the dog to a vet. Bemax or All-Bran,

sprinkled on the food daily, will supply roughage, the lack of which is the cause of this condition.

Arthritis
Old dogs can get this or it can be the result of broken bones. Feed Junior asprin for the pain; half a tablet night and morning, and keep the dog warm and dry.

Bad Breath
Decayed and dirty teeth and other mouth infections are the main cause, but worms, stomach disorders and kidney trouble are also causes. Dogs will usually take in chlorophyll – in the form of grass and green vegetables – to keep their breath clean. Charcoal biscuits will help the stomach disorders.

Balantitis
This appears as a discharge at the top of the dog's penis. Antibiotics and an antiseptic douch given in a jam jar is the best treatment.

Baldness
This is sometimes due to a hormone deficiency, sometimes to dietary factors, but worse, to infectious skin conditions such as mange. Old dogs lose their hair like old men and, although the loss can be halted, it cannot be cured. If baldness is infectious, strict attention to hygiene and daily medical baths and applications are necessary. Yeast and seaweed concentrate are good for coat conditioning.

Bee Stings
Remove sting with tweezers and apply blue bag or bicarbonate of soda and water paste, or an anti-histamine cream or spray. The bicarbonate is better for the mouth, tongue, lips and eyes.

Bleeding
Most bleeding can be slowed with a simple compress but, in more severe cases, a pressure bandage may be necessary. Place a thick pad over the bleeding wound and bind round with a bandage firmly, but not as tightly as a tourniquet which must be very tight to stem the heavier flow from an artery. The tourniquet is the action of a stick or pencil twisted through a loop until it is tight enough to stop the bleeding. Then it must be released at once; it should not be applied for more than ten minutes.

Broken Bones
While in the state of shock (qv), put a restraining muzzle on the dog so

that the vet will be able to examine him without a fight on his hands. If possible, don't move the dog and get the vet quickly so the bone can be set and put into splints at once. If he has to be taken to the vet, move him on a tray or piece of flat wood.

Burns

For fire and heat burns, soak in a solution of bicarbonate of soda and water – ¾lb. to a quart – and pour it over the burned area repeatedly. Don't use cotton wool; a piece of clean sheeting is best. Make a pad with the solution soaking it and tie round the burn and keep it moist by pouring more solution from the jug. A burn on the leg will respond to placing the limb in a bucket of iced water and keeping it there for twenty minutes. This will reduce the pain even before the vet arrives. Vaseline should be used in the last resort to keep out the air and a gauze dressing applied. Treat for shock (*qv*).

Cancer

A lot of important work is being done by a group of veterinary surgeons in Cambridge with equipment that has been modified for use on animals to treat cancers of the skin, etc. Up until now cancer has usually meant the death-knell as nobody knows what pain a dog suffers with cancer and it is wrong to keep a dog alive for your own satisfaction when he may be suffering.

Car Sickness

Never feed within eight hours of a long car journey if the dog is prone to sickness. Proprietary travel pills can be used if need be, but a drink of milk and glucose just before starting off usually sees most dogs all right. Travelling in a crate sometimes overcomes sickness and it does help to keep the car clean. A boiled marrow bone to chew and a comfortable cushion makes the idea of car travel more attractive.

Chills

Chills can cause stomach colic, shivering and a general out-of-sorts feeling. It is usually caused by sitting still for long periods in wet grass, after bathing or being in draughts. A bed raised nine inches off the ground is usually out of floor draughts.

Choking

Jack Russells often get caught up in a hole and have to bite their way out of trouble. Sometimes he is found with pieces of root stuck down his throat and they have to be hooked out quickly. Choking on bones or any other obstruction is best dealt with by holding the dog upside down and keeping his tongue depressed to let as much air as possible in the windpipe.

Chorea

This is a nervous twitching which is the result of hard pad and distemper. Treat as for nerves and muscular spasm. A good conditioner and sedatives are a help. Skullcap is a good remedy for nervous disorders in powder or tablet form.

Cleft Palate

A condition to look for in new born puppies who, because they can't suck properly cry in a most pitiful way even while they are trying to suck. When the roof of the mouth is examined it will be found — sometimes only tiny clefts that would hardly be thought to upset the pups proper feeding and large clefts reaching from behind the gum to the base of the tongue. Unless these clefts are spotted at the earliest possible moment the pup will be unable to suck properly and will die in a matter of days. A vet treated a Chihuahua and she was able to survive by being hand fed until the stitches healed up, but as a general rule such pups are best put to sleep. Your vet will do this for you.

Coccidiosis

This is a bacterial infection of the intestines and is the most usual cause of diarrhoea in a puppy when it refuses to respond to the usual treatment. This needs veterinary treatment and a course of antibiotics. It can be a killer but in any case greatly lowers the dog's resistance.

Conjunctivitis

Eyes can get irritated by dirt being scratched into them and by dogs pushing their way in the earths and rabbit holes. Tearing through hedgerows can scratch and damage the eyes too and the dust can cause very bad inflammation. Bathe the eyes in a mild solution of boracic and water. If the condition persists, get some eye ointment from the vet.

Constipation

If fed the right food, this rarely troubles terriers except in times of whelping or if the diet is not laxative enough. A good safe remedy is rhubarb tablets for older dogs, but it is safer to give milk of magnesia to puppies and pregnant bitches.

Convulsions

It is most frightening to watch as the dog writhes and jerks most violently, works his legs furiously and foams at the mouth making howling and screeching barking noises. He should be allowed to let the attack run its course and not be touched or talked to. Brain damage as the result of severe illness, such as distemper or the symptoms of some sorts of poisoning, should be suspected. Always consult your vet.

Cystitis

A very painful condition of the bladder which requires flushing out with plenty of water given to drink and a bland diet. Pearl barley boiled in the drinking water is good and fish or white meat only, because the eating of red meat, eggs, cheese and such produces a very acid urine which burns terribly. Masses of water is really the answer.

Demodectic Mange

Also known as Follicular. It is a mite which burrows inside the actual hair follicle. It first attacks the head and then all the rest of the body. Hair is lost and pus and blood form scabs. A drug is available which penetrates the hair follicles from within and destroys the mite. Other remedies are cheaper but less effective. Only a skin scraping can identify the condition and no time should be lost in starting treatment. This disease is not passed on to humans.

Diabetes Mellitus

This is a disease that is found in all breeds. It is more common in middle aged or older females. It is a condition in which the body chemistry has been altered by a chain of events that has led to a deficiency of insulin. Early signs are increased consumption of water, increased urination, increased appetite and considerable weight loss, the dog may vomit and have diarrhoea. If untreated the dog could go into a coma and die. This disease cannot be cured but can be kept under control by the injection of insulin.

Diarrhoea

This should never be overlooked as it is often a symptom of more serious complaints such as distemper and hepatitis, etc. The vet should be consulted if early remedies fail to effect a cure, or if there is blood in the motion. Sometimes diarrhoea is only caused by change of diet or scene. Kaolin is an effective remedy and feeding rice until the condition improves is the best answer.

Distemper

Nursing a case of this dreaded killer is the surest way I know of convincing the disbelieving of the importance of compulsory vaccination against this very terrible disease. It proclaims itself in so many different ways to start with that it is only recognised by its sad aftermath. If a dog, especially when a puppy, shows signs of running eyes and nose, accompanied by a hard dry cough, vomiting, diarrhoea and loss of appetite it is better to consult a vet quickly. Isolate the puppy – don't take him to the surgery and infect all the other dogs there. Meningitis, permanent loss of enamel on the teeth (called 'distemper teeth'), chorea and shaking fits, convulsions and many other chronic conditions can affect him for the rest of his life.

Drowning

The most important thing is to get all the water out of the dog's lungs as quickly as possible. Most dogs take to water easily and Jack Russells are splendid swimmers as a rule. Pull the tongue forward and hold him up by his hind legs to let the fluid drain out. Apply artificial respiration with the dog on its side; apply rhythmic pressure on his chest to get the breathing going again.

Ears

Tips of ears often get sore and split or hard and swollen. Warm some vaseline and coconut oil, mix together with some flowers of sulphur and rub into place until healed up and ears are soft again.

Ear Canker

A mite in the ear can cause the greatest distress to any dog. Dogs with lots of hair in their ears, such as spaniels, terriers and poodles, are prone to ear canker as once the mite is in, it cannot get out. The dog will hold its head on one side and give very gentle scratches at it and often make little cries. A very obnoxious smell is also a symptom. The hair must be removed with finger and thumb, and dry healing powder, which contains a small quantity of iodoform, inserted to kill the mite. This is the quickest way to give relief, clear up any unpleasant discharge and soothe the inflamed skin.

Eclampsia

Already mentioned (page 133), it affects bitches in lactation. An injection of calcium borogluconate at the earliest possible moment will bring her round miraculously. The puppies should be taken from the bitch and hand-fed.

Epilepsy and Fits

Dogs are not aware of their actions when under the throes of these conditions. Keep the dog in a darkened room, very quiet and send for the vet who will inject a sedative. An ice bag on the top of the head will help soothe the dog and an increased supply of Vit. B complex will help build up his condition. If fits persist, the vet usually recommends that the dog is put down.

Euthanasia

A Jack Russell that has lived an active, useful life will have no pleasure in sitting around the house waiting for death to relieve him of a distressing illness or just of sheer old age. You owe him the benefit of an easy and swift finish to life that now holds little joy and perhaps great discomfort and even pain. Today's method is for the vet to inject an extra large dose of anaesthetic into him so that instead of being made unconscious for surgery, he goes into such a deep sleep that he will never wake up again. If you hold him in your arms while the vet gives the injection, you will feel that you have stood by him to the end.

Eye Damage

In case of serious damage to an eye while out hunting such as being pierced by a gorse needle or bramble or having a twig scratch the surface of an eye the best thing to do is to spit into it copiously and keep on filling the eye with spit. I was told to do this by a doctor who was sitting at the ring when my little poodle jumped up and the wire bristle of the grooming brush pierced his eye. I did as instructed and the dog stopped screaming and didn't even have a mark on his eye. It is something to do with replacing enzymes. If the eye is injured by sand or brick dust becoming imbedded in it hold the head steady and pour castor oil into the affected eye. Hold it for as long as possible when the grit should move to the corner to be easily removed. If it still remains imbedded fill the eye again and brush gently with a piece of cotton wool. (I have used a budgie feather quite effectively after all else had failed).

Eye Ulcer

If the eye swells up and an ulcer appears fill the eye with cod liver oil — the refined type given to young babies — and keep the dog in the pitch dark, only letting him excercise after dark. Keep this up for six to eight weeks or until the ulcer has disappeared and no scar will be left.

Fleas

The kind of life Jack Russells lead puts them in close contact with the chief flea carriers — rabbits, hedgehogs, rats and squirrels. Black 'grit' in the coat next to the skin is a sure sign fleas are present, and the dog should be dusted with a flea powder and his bedding also treated. Severe cases benefit from special insecticidal baths. Alugan, a new and effective product, is obtainable from your vet and will keep fleas away for two weeks after one application of the spray. A concentrated dusting powder is available in 20 gram sachets which can be used in a bath for your dog or in solution, using a hand-held spray, on his bedding and the household environment.

Gastro-Enteritis

This is a very serious form of internal infection that needs veterinary treatment with antibiotics and very careful nursing. A no-fat diet, light food and curtailing drink are advisable.

Hard Pad

This is thought to be caused by the distemper virus and is equally as dangerous. The pads, nose and tips of the ears harden, and speckling is seen on the inside of the ear flaps and in the groin. It is most important that all puppies are inoculated against hard pad.

Harvest Bugs

These are often found in the folds of the ears of country dogs used to running through corn fields, and look like tiny grains of bright red sand. Rubbing the skin with paraffin and milk mixture will help kill the mites.

Heart Disease

Dogs can live for a long time with a damaged heart as long as they have the right drugs and careful nursing. Many old dogs overcome the condition, but the possibility of death is never far away. Digitalis is much in use and Vit. E is believed to have a restorative effect on the heart. It has been found that dogs who are given wheatgerm as a daily part of the diet do not suffer from heart trouble.

Heat Stroke

Dogs should never be shut up in cars or anywhere there is no current of air. This causes a high rise in temperature and it must be reduced as soon as possible. A bath of icy cold water and his body completely immersed in it, holding his head above it, is the quickest way. If there is not a container big enough to plunge him in, keep pouring very cold water over him and keep a fan blowing cold air on him for a couple of hours.

Hepatitis

Canine Virus Hepatitis is the full name of this killer disease. It is so serious that puppies can be infected through the umbilical cord before they are even born. The dog should be vaccinated against this virus at the same time as against distemper. It affects the liver and many puppies who fade out at an early age are found to be victims of it. The first signs are loss of appetite and an apparent soreness of the abdomen, and later maybe conjunctivitis but on the whole, the symptoms are so difficult to detect that a dog may be dead before anyone realises what he is suffering from.

Hernia

This affects the navel or the groin. It is sometimes soft and harmless but if hard to the touch, an operation is advised.

Hook Worms

In certain countries these can be a major problem but in the U.K. they are mostly found in groups of kennelled dogs such as foxhounds and greyhounds. These worms are very small, about 12 mm in length and bent into a hook shape. They can cause anaemia through their blood sucking action, but can be controlled by a larger dose of roundworm tablets.

Hysteria

Screaming fits can be the result of distemper or a certain substance found in agene – a whitening agent in bread making. It appears to be catching so the sooner it is stopped, the better. Get the dog into a darkened room until the attack subsides and keep him quiet for some days, under sedation if necessary.

Interdigital Cysts

These are very painful swellings between the toes and may be caused by sharp grass seeds penetrating the skin in these places. These become intermittent and are very painful, causing the dog to lick and aggrevate the condition. Hot poultices or Morrison paste – Epsom salts and glycerine – are good remedies.

Kennel Cough

This is a very contagious condition that spreads quickly when dogs are in a confined space – such as boarding kennels and indoor dog shows. Do not take the dog to the vet where he will infect others, but ask the vet for antibiotics. You must complete the course recommended by the vet. Local treatment can be a children's cough linctus which will ease the coughing but not cure it.

Lead Poisoning

This is caused by licking paint or chewing anything containing lead. Only lead-free paints should be used where a dog is about. Use mustard and water or salt and water as an emetic or a piece of washing soda pushed down the throat. If the dog seems in great agony, pour warmed black treacle down its throat. A general sort of antidote can be kept in the medicine chest made up of two parts charcoal, one part magnesium oxide, one part Kaolin and one part tannic acid. This powder should be mixed at the rate of four heaped tablespoons of antidote to a ½ pint of warm water. Get as much of this as possible down the dog's throat.

Leptospiral Jaundice
Two injections at monthly intervals can give protection against this rat-borne disease which severely attacks the liver. Symptoms can be mistaken for distemper, but signs of haemorrhage producing black stools are characteristic of this infection which is transmitted by the rat through its urine. Regular booster jabs are recommended.

Lice
Lice are skin parasites which are much harder to get rid of than fleas. A strong louse powder can cure them if the smell isn't too repellent. It takes a strong substance to remove them as they stick their heads into the skin. Benzyl benzoate is effective and a mixture of sulphur, paraffin and mineral oil can be applied. A very strong anti-insecticidal bath should be given after attempts have been made to get rid of the lice. This bath should be repeated every few days.

Mange
Sarcoptic or red mange is caused by a mite that burrows under the skin, lays its eggs and emerges a few days later ready to repeat the whole process. It is a most serious and irritating condition and made worse by the dog biting and scratching itself. The treatment must follow the life cycle of the mite and as it is just as likely to affect humans in the form of scabies, no time should be lost in starting treatment. In a longer-haired dog, clip the coat down to the skin and bathe in Tetmosl or Kur-Mange and leave in the coat. Two days later, repeat the bath to kill the female as the mites emerge and three days later again give the dog a bath which takes care of the eggs as they hatch. If any mites or eggs are found, a repeat performance must be given and continued until there is no further sign of trouble. Benzyl benzoate lotion is a good cure. *See also Demodectic Mange* and *Baldness*. Your vet will have up to date treatments.

Mastitis
This is an infection of the udder which becomes very red, swollen and painful. Veterinary treatment is needed urgently and antibiotics must be given without delay. The pups should be removed as the milk will be lethal and hand-feeding must be resorted to until the bitch recovers.

Meningitis
The high fever encountered in this condition leaves the brain so damaged that recovery is doubtful. Complete sedation is the only hope.

I have cured it but it meant keeping the dog under a drug for a long time. It was quite unconscious and was drip-fed on a saline drip, using hydrolised protein or glucose.

Metritis
This acute inflammation of the womb resulting in very high fever and imminent death. A complete removal of the whole womb (hysterectomy) is advisable.

Muscular Rheumatism
A very painful and sudden condition, which seems to affect the hindquarters. Quarter and half doses of Junior asprin, night and morning, seem to help the pain. You should keep the dog warm and out of draughts. Always dry him – especially his hindquarters – when he comes in out of the wet.

Nephritis
This is a chronic disorder of the kidneys which used to affect eighty per cent of dogs who passed eight years of age. There are two types: non-uremic, the less dangerous, and uremic which causes great loss of weight, a most unpleasant ammoniac smell and total apathy. Treatment is unlikely to effect a cure but the non-uremic kind can be helped by giving the dog plenty of water to drink – especially barley water – and a bland diet.

Nose
Dry cracked skin on the nose responds to vaseline being smeared on it regularly. This condition is improved when more fat or oil is added to the diet.

Obesity
This is unlikely to affect a Jack Russell, unless he is indiscriminately fed. A very restricted diet is necessary and a reduction in carbohydrates. One day's complete fasting a week can work wonders.

Otitis
An infection of the ear, this entails the need for competent professional treatment as it can result in deafness. A grey or yellowish discharge is seen exuding from the ear.

Parvo Virus
Parvo virus is the most serious and devastating disease any dog can get and it either kills or leaves an enlarged heart and other serious malfunctions. The symptoms of Parvo virus are vomitting and diar-

rhoea, usually with blood in them, followed by a big weight loss, dehydration and then death. The very latest Parvo virus vaccine, Nobi-Vac Parvo C & DHP, is a tremendous breakthrough as with it the puppy can be safely vaccinated at a very early age and it can be used with complete safety in pregnant bitches. It has no adverse effects on fertility.

Prostrate Gland Enlargement

This condition causes constipation as the prostate presses against the wall of the rectum. Castration causes the gland to waste away and is an effective solution to the condition which can occur after six years in the male dog.

Rabies

Known as hydrophobia. Due to the right quarantine laws in this country, we have been able to control this dreaded disease even though it is rife in parts of Europe and in North and South America where bats and foxes are thought to be its chief sources of infection. Vaccination against it from about the age of six months has proved good protection. The disease is transmitted through a rabid dog biting another animal or human. If immediate attention isn't given, the victim is wracked with violent spasmodic convulsions and dies in a very short time.

Rickets

This is the result of a calcium deficiency in puppyhood. The addition of Vit. A and D in bone-meal will help matters so long as phosphates are included as well.

Ringworm

Round bald patches with a thin red line denote this condition which can be controlled with applications of Stockholm Tar or linseed oil and creosote. Use a long-handled paint brush, as the fungus can affect humans just as much. Strict attention should be given to the burning of all bedding, spraying of woodwork and floors, etc. with the strongest possible fungus killer.

Roundworm (Toxocara Canis)

The most common worm and puppies are often already infected in their mother's womb as the worm is carried through the blood stream. It can also be transferred via the mother's milk or other puppies' faeces or infected dogs' faeces. Dose with Endorid wormer made by Beecham's every six months and don't let dogs, especially nursing bitches, lick children. Train your dog to use the gutter not the park.

Scalding

If a pan of boiling liquid is spilt on your dog, stand him in the sink or bath and keep on soaking and drenching him with cold water to wash away the hot liquid. The same applies to corrosive chemicals which can be washed away and diluted. Treat for shock (*qv*).

Scurf

A dessertspoonfull of salad oil taken daily is a good way of treating this condition as it is a sign of dietary deficiency. Various baths are also effective.

Senility

A Jack Russell Terrier can be expected to live to thirteen or fourteen years. There is a treatment for senile dogs, Debenal, which is a kind of sulphonamide. Daily doses are necessary or the body will revert to its senile state and it takes a couple of weeks to take effect.

Shock

As the result of road and other accidents and in the case of burns, scalds, severe stings and snake bites, cover the dog completely with a blanket and put a hot water bottle, if available, at each side or place him on an electric blanket or heated pad. The patient *must* be kept warm. If the gums are pale and the heart beat slow, the dog may be haemorrhaging. Give him a glucose saline by mouth or, if trained, give via a hypodermic syringe. The saline is made from one dessertspoonful of glucose and one level teaspoonful of salt to a pint of water. Very sweet tea or coffee can be given, but do not give alcohol or other stimulants of that nature.

Tape Worm

Fully grown tape worm may be one metre or more in length. Tape worm have a flat segmented body and a small head and they attach themselves to the gut wall. To complete their life cycle, their eggs must pass out in the faeces either singly or in chains. Re-infestation occurs when the tape worm passes into a host animal which can be a flea. A dog swallows a flea and he gets tape worm. Keep your dog free from fleas and he won't get tape worm so easily.

Tartar on Teeth

The accumulation of tartar means the dog hasn't enough hard chewing on bones and biscuits to keep his teeth clean. Very severe cases will need attention with a tooth scraper.

Teething Rash
Found on stomach and inside puppies' legs. Cover spots with gentian violet and dose with Milk of Magnesia or similar. Feed bonemeal to hasten teething.

Temperature
A dog's temperature is normally 101.4 Farenheit. A one or two degree variation can be treated with suspicion of ill-health but any more each way and veterinary help is required.

Ticks
These are found where sheep are kept, and they attach themselves to the skin and suck the blood and in doing so expand to a tremendous extent. Surgical spirit applied on a piece of cotton wool will make them release their hold and they should be burned immediately with a match or thrown in the fire. Dogs should be checked for ticks at regular intervals: round the ears and armpits are often the most popular place for ticks.

Tonsillitis
Quite often found in the dog sometimes needing removal of tonsils. Treat with antibiotics and keep warm until temperature is normal. Feed a liquid diet or jelly until throat soreness is gone.

Tumors
Swellings that can appear on all parts of the body. They may be benign and can be removed under anaesthetic. If thought to be cancerous it is best to put the dog to sleep painlessly as it is impossible to judge just how much pain the patient may be suffering.

Vomiting
A means of expelling contents of the stomach: not an illness but a sign all is not well. Yellow bile in the vomit is a sign of liver upset from too much fat. Any blood in the vomit requires urgent veterinary advice.

Warts
There are excrescences that appear on the skin of ageing dogs. They can be cauterised by the vet or treated with daily applications of castor oil which will dry them up.

Wasp Stings
The stings are not left behind. Treat the place with vinegar, lemon or onion juice and spray on pain killer.

SUGGESTED CONTENTS OF FIRST AID CUPBOARD

Many of the things listed below will be in the family medicine cupboard already. Unless you have quite a number of dogs, you may not feel it is necessary to have all these things and certainly most of them are obtainable from the chemist or your vet.

Anti-histamine spray
Asprin, Junior
Baking Soda or Bicarbonate of
    Soda
Bandages
Benzyl Benzoate
Blue Bag
Burn Ointment
Castor Oil
Charcoal
Cornflour
Cotton Wool
Disinfectant
Docking Scissors
Eye Lotion and Ointment
Flea Comb
Friar's Balsam
Glucose
Hairbrush
Hound Glove
Hydrogen of Peroxide
Insecticidal Shampoo and
    Powder

Iodine
Kaolin
Milk of Magnesia
Mineral Oil
Mustard
Nail Clippers
Permanganate of Potash
Rhubarb Tablets
SA 37 Vitamin and Mineral
    Supplement
Salt
Savlon
Scissors
Soda
Sulphurated Potash Flowers of
    Sulphur
Thermometer (special animal
    one)
Vaseline
Vinegar
Witch Hazel
Worm Tablets

Do remember to destroy old medicines. They have usually lost their healing power but retain any poison compounds.

11　The End of the Beginning

Correspondence taken from The Field
Mrs Violet Thomas met an elderly lady in the lounge of a Barnstaple hotel in 1950 and got into conversation with her about the smooth-coated Jack Russell Terrier she had with her. The old lady said she was John Russell's granddaughter and had often stayed with him and hunted with him and his dogs; and *all* his terriers were broken-coated, whatever their shape and size. The old lady died soon afterwards and Mrs Thomas surmised that she would have to have been the daughter of John Russell's only surviving son (the other having died in infancy) John Bury Russell who died just after his father. Mrs Violet Thomas, from Staplegrove Manor, Taunton, said she wished she had had more conversation with the very charming old lady. Later, Mr Vernon Bartlett wrote to *The Field* in reply:
'Mrs Violet Thomas is absolutely correct. There never was a smooth-coated Parson Jack Russell. All were and are broken-coated or rough but not 'wiry'. The size and shape were and are "That of a fully grown vixen".'
Russell's own standard is 14in. at the withers and weight about 16lb.
Apropos of this, Betty Chichester of Barnstaple in North Devon wrote to say that she understood from local knowledge that the Rev. J. Russell would breed from *anything* the right size and shape whether mongrel or pure-bred.

Margot Thompson of Atherstone in Warwickshire wrote that the Rev. Jack Russell never bred a terrier that was not a 'working terrier'. She mentions a breed called Devon's Pride and also stated that the Midland Working Terrier Club had been formed to look after the interests of the working terrier.

Margot Thompson later sent a photograph of a smooth short-legged terrier that is of a good working strain and typifies the terrier most often associated with working.
To these three ladies Vernon Bartlett replied:
'I must contradict Betty Chichester (May 6th, 1965) in what she said. The memoirs of the Rev. John Russell (1795-1883) were published six months after Russell's death by his old friend Davies. Save for the final few pages notifying his death, all the book had been submitted to Russell by Davies for approval.

'Betty Chichester would seem to be wrong. Russell *carefully* [the italics are mine] bred his fox terriers using much good stuff from the shires to improve the local material – the old, game Devonshire terrier. The immortal Trump, that wonderful fox terrier bitch, is the outstanding example. No shred of evidence can be produced to dispute this.

'Violet Thomas is absolutely right to say there never was a smooth one.

'Coming to Margot Thompson, I find myself with every courtesy, very largely disagreeing. She is correct in her statement that Russell never bred a terrier that was not a working fox terrier. He was a leading fox terrier judge as the dogs appeared a hundred or more years ago and not as they mostly become from 1880 onwards. The real Parson Jack Russell was and remains a working terrier.

'The newly formed Midland Working Terrier Club is well-named and I wish it great success. Members must call their dogs working or hunt terriers unless they have some broken-haired fox terriers the size of a fully-grown vixen and around 14in. and 16lb. when they would be entitled to call them Parson Jack Russell Terriers after entry to fox.

'Margot Thompson is utterly wrong in writing of a breed Devon's Pride. The parson Jack Russell Terrier was never a breed. It is, always was, and I hope will always remain, a type of working fox terrier. The photograph Margot Thompson sent is typical of the popular misconception of a Jack Russell Terrier.'

A few editions later, Mr Vernon Bartlett of Exmouth, Devon, wrote:
'It warms my heart to learn that the *true* Jack Russell Terrier can still be found and can hold his own with the more popular and more showy tiny smooth types but now a Jack Russell owned by a Miss Susan Hurrell of Exmouth won a 1st Prize at the Culmstock Otter Hounds Working Terrier Show. I admire all working terriers and the courage of some of the tiny 10in. 10lb. smooths and roughs is beyond question.'

Mrs Betty Smith of Kinnersley, Hereford, wrote:
'Since my book on the Jack Russell Terrier was published, I have received letters from all over the world sending photgraphs and they all refer to their terriers as Jack Russells and the photographs can all be recognised as belonging to the same strain. I have requests for tiny types from Cape Province in South Africa where dogs always grow bigger than their antecedents. They only want smooths as ticks are liable to infest long coats.'

Mr J. Fuller of Sidmouth, Devon, asked:
'Why doesn't *The Field* publish a photograph of a "Real" Jack Russell as Margot Thompson's picture is a *mongrel* with bull terrier blood which the Parson condemned over and over again?' The Editor replied that they hadn't a suitable photograph in their possession.

The beginning of this breed was due to the hard work of the Rev. John Russell and however much it has meandered in looks from its original form, the aim is the same as that sporting old gentleman's – to produce a terrier for specific requirements. Today, people's requirements are slightly different and so the terrier has been altered to fit, always bearing in mind that the Rev. John Russell was born in 1795, about eighty years before the inception of the Kennel Club in 1873.

Many of today's breeds were in their early stages then, if they existed at all, and if a study is made of the drawings of A. Baker, for instance, in 'Stonehenge's' *Dogs of the British Isles* (1886), it will be seen that John Russell's terriers were much nearer the then wire-haired fox terrier than to the present-day ones. As they were not registered with the Kennel Club, there was no necessity for them to conform to a laid-down pattern like the wire-haired fox terriers have done, and so there is a far greater divergence of type. The fact that the breed, as it is seen today, is still recognisable is to be commended. There is no knowing how it would turn out if given the benefit of Kennel Club recognition and the consequent purity of breeding.

It is felt that no better conclusion can be drawn than to end this book with the obituary to the Rev. John Russell which appeared in the *Kennel Club Gazette* of May 1883, a month after his death on 28 April in his eighty-eighth year and a short time before the death of his son Col. John Bury Russell J.P. of the North Devon Militia.

IN MEMORIAM – *The Rev. John Russell*

Though fiction in a past generation gave us a Parson Adams [Parson Abraham Adams, a character in Fielding's *Joseph Andrews*], there is no likelihood of a nearer prototype of that worthy than the kind old clergyman who passed quietly away just ten days ago. The resemblance between the country parson of the novelist and the Rev. John Russell ends, however, at the point where both are seen to exercise an influence upon all those with whom they came in contact, and an honesty of purpose to be constantly helping others out of scrapes or troubles. This was the character of John Russell but he was a greater gentleman than Parson Adams, and his journey through life may be looked upon as an odd sort of mixture between the old-fashioned parson, the country gentleman and the courtier. In his parish, he was the adviser and friend of his flock, at cover side or at the agricultural meeting; he was hearty and well met with every one, and in the hall or the palace he was polished and affable to a degree. It is no wonder, therefore, that he was a universal favourite, from prince to the peasant, and it is possible that no one has ever surpassed him as an arbitrator and peacemaker in every sort of circle. He would travel third-class from Devonshire to Yorkshire for no other purpose, and whether in bringing together broken ties or preaching a charity sermon, he had a way of his own of reaching the heart that few could equal and none could surpass.

Born a sportsman, he never thought it incompatable with duty to join in every sort of legitimate sport and pastime; and besides being the most genuine foxhunter in the country, it was by no means unusual to see his well-known figure at Ascot or Stockbridge, or on the box of a friend's drag in the coaching season. There was no cant or hum-bug about John Russell: he performed the duties of his religious profession better than the majority of clergymen, and he was ever ready to join in anything to promote sport or fellowship amongst sportsmen. The writer of these lines asked him, when the Kennel Club was established, to join as a member, and he was quite delighted with the idea, and has been a member ever since. It will be remembered that Mr Russell judged the Fox Terriers at the Crystal Palace for the Club in 1875, and although the old gentleman was not altogether at home with all the requirements of the modern fox terrier, he was greatly pleased with all he saw at the show. Mr Russell's own breed of fox terriers were wire-haired, and his great aversion were those that had in them any sign of a bull cross. A real fox terrier, he would say, is not meant to murder, and his intellegence should always keep him from such a crime. Thus, he boasted that the best he ever had, never tasted blood to his knowledge, but they could not lose their way, and that their eye to country and memory was so great that, as soon as hounds were out of cover, some of his terriers had gone ten miles, and reached well-known earths in time to stop a fox from entering a destination that he had been making for. This Mr Russell thought, was the highest character that could be found in a terrier and he would have none that hesitated to go to ground, but he liked them to tease or worry a fox rather than to kill or fight it. He said his terriers worked for the pack, and knew as well as he did what they were wanted for. The Jack Russell terrier was hardly as big as the modern show terrier; in working condition the dogs would not be more than 15lb., and many of them hardly that, and five and twenty years ago they formed a very distinct type. Since that time they have been crossed on to other strains and their uniformity has been probably lost, though they live in all the descendents of Foiler. Mr Russell started his breed at Oxford when he was eighteen, something like seventy years ago, and he had his pedigrees that he could trace to from that time. As the oldest fox terrier breeder in England Mr Russell's connection with the Kennel Club was an honour to that body, and we personally regret the loss of a very old friend, and that a thousand followed him to his grave that were nearly all of them sportsmen shows that our slight contribution, as well as any others written by staunch friends and admirers, is largely shared in sentiment to the memory of the Rev. John Russell.

Appendix 1

Some Useful Addresses

The Jack Russell Terrier Club of Great Britain, Secretary: Mrs Thelma Loomes, Primrose Cottage, West Street, Dormandsland, Nr Lingfield, Surrey

The Parson Jack Russell Terrier Club, Secretary: Ruth Wilford, Pirton House, Pirton, Wadborough, Worcestershire WR8 9EJ Tel. 0905 821444

Breeds Record Officer: Mrs Sheila Atter, Little Owl End, Church Lane, East Kirby, Spilsbury, Lincolnshire PE23 4BX Tel. 0790 3289

The Shires Jack Russell Terrier Club, Secretary: Mrs R. A. Copping Tel. (Tadley) 07356 6352

Appendix 2

The Parson Jack Russell Terrier Club

In 1983 the Parson Jack Russell Terrier Club was reformed in order to try to get the Jack Russell Terrier registered with the Kennel Club as all attempts by the other Jack Russell clubs to get recognition had failed. This was probably because there were far too many different types and coat textures and sizes to be taken into account before a breed could have been derived. Many of the so-called Jack Russell Terriers were of poor type, unsound in body, too wide in chest and of the wrong colour. Many who may have looked all right were cross-bred and produced mongrel offspring.

The Parson Jack Russell Terrier Club however has only one size and one size only: it is 14″ high, 14″ along the back and 14 lbs in weight.

The Parson Jack Russell Terrier Club was originally formed at the turn of the century and was given the blueprint laid down by the Reverend John Russell. It was affiliated to the Kennel Club. Part of the reason for its revival is to counter the threat to the Parson Jack Russell Terrier from the smaller terrier types that are being promoted as Jack Russell Terriers. The aim of the Club is the eventual recognition by the Kennel Club of the Parson Jack Russell Terrier, whilst still preserving its working ability.

Ridley Redstart bred by Mrs S. M. Atter is an excellent example of the reformed Parson Jack Russell Club terrier – a modern version of Trump with very similar markings.

The Breed Standard of the Parson Jack Russell Terrier Club

Characteristics: The Jack Russell is essentially a working terrier and should be bold and confident at all times. Nervousness, cowardice or over aggression are to be discouraged.

Head and Skull: Should be flat, moderately broad, gradually narrowing to the eyes. Little stop should be apparent. The length from stop to occiput should be slightly longer than that from stop to nose.

Ears: Small, V-shaped, dropping forward and carried close to the head.

Eyes: Dark and almond-shaped.

Jaws: Strong and muscular.

Teeth: Scissor bite.

Nose: Coloured black.

Neck: Clean and muscular, of good length, gradually widening to the shoulders. (The terrier, when working underground, should be able to extend its neck to enable its mouth to reach beyond its paws.)

Shoulders: Long and sloping, well laid back and clearly cut at the withers.

Chest: Of moderate depth, capable of being spanned, by average sized hands, behind the shoulders. (Approximate measurement 14″–15″.)

Back: Strong and straight, the length in comparison to the height of the terrier to give a balanced image. The loin slightly arched.

Tail: Straight, strong and set high. Length complementing the body while providing a good handhold.

Forelegs: Strong and straight with joints in correct alignment. Elbows hanging perpendicular to the body, working free of the sides.

Hindquarters: Strong and muscular with good angulation and bend of stifle. Hocks near the ground, giving plenty of drive. Looking from behind the hocks must be straight.

Feet: Cat-like.

Gait: Movement to be free, lively and well co-ordinated with straight action in front and behind.

Coat: Rough, a trifle wiry, or smooth. Dense with belly and undersides not bare.

Colour: Predominatly white, with black or tan markings, or a combination of these, i.e. tricolour.

Height: 14″.

Note: Male animals to have two apparently normal testicles fully descended into the scrotum. Scars and injuries resulting from work should not prejudice a terrier's chance in the show-ring unless they interfere with its movement and ability to work.

Bibliography

Ash, Edward C., M.R.A.C., *The Practical Dog Book* (Simkin Marshall 1930)

Badcock, Lt. Col. G.H., *Disobedient Dogs* (Herbert Jenkins 1933)

Barton, F.T., M.R.C.V.S., *Our Dog & All About Them* (Jarrold & Sons 1910)

Bryant, Sir Arthur, *Jimmy, the Dog in my Life* (1960)

Castle, Sidney & Marples, Theo, *Monograph on the Fox Terrier* (Our Dogs 1915)

Chance, Michael, *Whose Dog Are You?* (John Murray 1938)

Cox, Major Harding, *Dogs and 'I'* (Hutchinson 1923)

Daglish, E. Fitch, *The Dog Breeders Manual* (J.M. Dent 1951)

Dalziel, Hugh, *British Dogs* (L. Upcott Gill 1881)

Dalziel, Hugh & Maxtee, J., *The Fox Terrier & All About it* (L. Upcott Gill 1899)

Davies, E.W.L., *Memoir of the Rev. John Russell* (Chatto & Windus 1882)

Dawson, Major A.J., *Everybody's Dog Book* (Collins 1922)

Fisher, Catherine, *The Dog* (Evans 1960)

Goldsmith, Oliver, M.D., *National History* Vol. I (Blackie 1852)

Hammond, S.T., *Practical Dog Training* (Forest & Stream 1885)

Heath, J.B., *Aids to Veterinary Nursing* (Balliere, Tindall & Cassell 1970)

Holmes, John, *The Choice & Training of the Family Dog* (Hutchinson 1957)

Hubbard, Clifford L.B., *Dogs in Britain* (Macmillan 1948)

Hubbard, Clifford L.B., *Observers Book of the Dog* (Warne 1948)

'Idstone', (Rev. Thomas Pearce), *The Dog* (Cassell 1872)

Judy, Will, *Training the Dog* (Judy Publishing 1933)

Kerr, Eleanor, *Hunting Parson* (Herbert Jenkins 1963)

Lee, Rawdon B., *The Fox Terrier* (Horace Cox 1889)

Lee, Sir Sidney, *The Life of Edward VII*

Leedham, Charles, *Care of the Dog* (Constable 1962)

Leighton, Robert, *The Book of the Dog* (Cassell)

Leighton, Robert, *The Complete Book of the Dog* (Cassell 1922)

Leighton, Robert, *Dogs & All About Them* (Cassell 1910)

Leighton, Robert, *Your Dog* (Cassell 1924)

Lloyd, William, *Hints on Dog Breaking* (Warne 1882)

Mayhew, Sewell & Cousins, *Dogs & Their Management* (Routledge 1939)

Mery, Fernand, *The Life History & Magic of the Dog* (Madison Square Press 1968)

Mulvany, Mollie, *All About Obedience Training* (Pelham Books 1973)

Pathfinder & Dalziel, *Breaking & Training Dogs* (L. Upcott Gill 1903)

Peake, Harry C., *Practical Dog Breeding* (Macmillan, New York, 1947)

Price, E.W., *History of Hunting* (Daniel Owen)

Price, E.W., *Horn & Hound in Wales & Adjoining Counties* (Daniel Owen 1881)

'Russell, Dan', *Jack Russell & His Terriers* (J.A. Allen 1979)

Sewell, A.J., M.R.C.V.S., *The Dog's Medical Dictionary* (Routledge 1923)

Smith, Betty, *Jack Russell Terrier*

Stampa, G.L., *In Praise of Dogs* (Muller 1948)

'Stonehenge', *Dogs of the British Isles* (The Field 1872)

Stranger, Joyce, *The Running Foxes* (Hammond & Hammond 1965)

Trevelyan, G.M., O.M., *Illustrated English Social History* (Longmans Green 1949)

Vesey-Fitzgerald, Brian, *The Book of the Dog* (Nicholson & Watson 1948)

Whates, H.R., *The Life & Times of King Edward VII* (Cassell)

Wood, E. Lindley, *Smooth Fox Terriers* (Foyles 1960)

Woodhouse, Barbara, *Dog Training My Way* (Woodhouse 1973)

also *The Kennel Club Stud Books* Vol. 1&2 (1874 & 1875), *Hutchinson's Popular Illustrated Dog Encyclopaedia* (1935), *The Field, Horse and Hound, Shooting Times, Countryside, Kennel Club Gazette*.

Index